GLOBAL TECTONICS
what every business needs to know

Fariborz Ghadar
Erik Peterson

This short monograph is dedicated to William A. Schreyer, whose support and guidance have made this project possible. Bill's strategic insight and capacity to effect change – across the private sector, academia, and the policy world – represent the kind of strategic leadership necessary to address the tectonic changes all around us.

TABLE OF CONTENTS

Global Trends: Introduction

Worldwide, CEOs and senior managers need to prepare their industries for Global Tectonic — the process by which developing trends in technology, nature, and society slowly revolutionize the business environment of the future. Much like the earth's tectonic plates, global trends are shifting the ground beneath our feet — unnoticed — and transforming our industrial and societal topography. Business executives easily and often overlook such gradual developments — that is, until a major seismic event shakes their corporate foundations.

In this project, we have identified 12 global trends that we believe will present the most formidable challenges to business leaders in the next 30 years. Developments in areas such as demography, infectious disease, resource degradation, economic integration, nanotechnology, information technology, international conflict, and governance will determine whether corporate strategies stay intact or unravel. These tectonic shifts will also determine whether industries have prepared for minor tremors or major earthquakes. When the dust settles, the tectonics will reveal the extent to which businesses have prepared for imminent change. Corporations have both the ability and the responsibility to foresee, to understand, and to adjust to these trends as they unfold.

We categorize tectonic shifts as societal, technological, and environmental. One set of global trends arises from the interactions of people with their environment. The global population is growing, cities are burgeoning, and these demographic changes impact resource management, health, and the quality of life for people and businesses around the world. Technology, another key tectonic driver, powers economic growth and development. Advances in biotechnology, nanotechnology, and information systems have enhanced global economic integration, fueling the "knowledge economy." A third set of trends describes shifts within the international system and civil society. The end of the Cold War sparked a new wave of democratization, economic integration, and governance that continues to transform the fundamentals of international business.

Many of these trends overlap in both degree and direction, which often-times serves to complicate the potential for industry to respond. For instance, the availability of land, labor, and critical inputs such as energy depends on trends in population growth, biotechnology, urbanization, and natural resource management. We also observe that the growth of the knowledge economy and enhanced economic integration have risen mainly from developments in the field of information technology. Given the interconnectivity and synergy between such trends, business leaders must interpret tectonic shifts on a case-by-case basis. Every business, regardless of its size or industry, must view day-to-day operations in light of these global developments.

Our report is intended to facilitate this type of analysis by clearly outlining global trends and their potential impact on international business. The evolution of global tectonics will be pivotal in CEOs' decision-making processes — both now and decades into the future.

Unveiling the trends that pose the greatest threat to long-term corporate operations has been an interesting and exciting challenge. This project has been enjoyable to complete, and we acknowledge with gratitude the entire Global Trends team for their dedication to this report, from its conception to its conclusion. Our journey to a final product consisted of several phases. At first, we identified the key issues and determined the framework of analysis for each trend. Our conversations with CEOs and senior managers across a variety of disciplines, such as manufacturing, services, finance, and marketing, helped us recognize individual and global business concerns. Investigating the views and opinions of these executives, we pinpointed the 12 trends we needed to cover in this booklet.

With a framework for analysis in place, we began the difficult task of researching and reporting on each trend. Research assistants Phillip Thompson and William Knauss, both undergraduate students in the Penn State Schreyer Honors College, did an excellent job of fact gathering, preliminary authoring, and research. Chen Lei demonstated outstanding dedication in the initial spade work and investigation as well as in the graphic design of data. This group gave the entire team a good head start on each of the trends, and their combined groundwork helped lay the foundation for the next phase of the project.

Team leaders Namrata Kripalani and Lauren Anderson then worked on what Thomas Friedman calls the "Arbitrage of Information" — taking complex concepts and reporting them in simple, comprehensive prose so that readers of all backgrounds, interests, and areas of expertise could benefit from the information. Namrata and Lauren have been the backbone of this project, giving both direction and clarity to potentially intractable subjects. Their dedication to quality, accuracy, and aesthetics brought this project to completion. We also owe our individual and collective thanks to Heather Spindler for her extensive contribution and research on nanotechnology, and her chapter edits. Beth Hardy has been tireless in her efforts to ensure the accuracy and timeliness of the data. We also thank Kate Delano Poorman for her editorial suggestions and work.

From its inception, this undertaking has been an insightful journey for the entire team. Several brainstorming sessions, followed by extensive research, fueled numerous discussions that formed the basis for an initial composition of each of the sections as well as the creation of graphs and data used to support the theories. Lauren and Namrata shared in innumerable rounds of research, documentation, and draft writing, as well as the initial graphic design. This project was unusually team oriented, and we can proudly say that it would be difficult to assign credit for a particular analysis to any one member of the team. They functioned incredibly well as a unit, finding value in constructive criticism, and working as a group to meet deadlines and project goals.

We are also indebted to the members of the advisory board of the Center for Global Business Studies, including: Michel Amsalem, Bill Davidson, Robert Hamilton, Robert Joyce, Laura Kohler, John Koo, Nirmal Pal, Yoon Park, William A. Schreyer, Mazen Snobar, Robert Svensk, and James Thomsen. They have all been very generous with their time and support. In particular, we are grateful for the videotaping provided by the board and for the guidance they have given on the project. In addition, our deep appreciation is extended to Marilyn Mitchell and Bruce Hwozdek from Seven Three Media for their design work and development of the multimedia CD, to Steven Infanti and Geoffrey Skadra for their editorial work and artistic polish, and to the Center for Global Business Studies' business manager, Nancy Dull, for her help to the entire research team in coordinating all the resources needed to complete this project.

At the very least, we hope our hard work and research will evoke discussions about the future of business. We urge you to debate our conclusions, to take our caveats to heart, and to engage in responsible business planning. Corporations that have prepared for the "earthquakes" we predict will not be shaken down. We trust that this project will stimulate preparation for the inevitable changes we now know as Global Tectonics.

Fariborz Ghadar
Erik Peterson

SECTION ONE

People
and
Environment

POPULATION TRENDS

CHAPTER
one

Shifts in the nature and rate of global population growth are the first of the major tectonic forces that we expect will shape the future business environment. Across the planet, demographic trends are transforming societies, modifying economic patterns, generating new economic and social dependencies, and altering geopolitical balances. How well businesses anticipate and adapt to these challenges will mean the difference between success and failure, opportunity and disappointment.

What are the main characteristics of the population changes that we can expect to see? The first and inescapable element is that the world population is rising quickly. It will likely increase from its current level of some 6.35 billion to some 7.8 billion by the year 2025, to some 8.8–9.1 billion by the year 2050.[1]

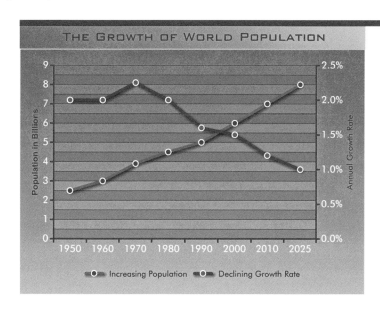

But as significant as these numbers may seem to be, a related factor is that our overall rate of global population growth is not increasing at all. Rather, it is decreasing — and decreasing rapidly. This is the second key dimension of this tectonic force now at work. In the late 1960s, when many analysts were concerned about the imminent "population explosion," the rate of growth across the world had already peaked. Since that point, it has dropped significantly — by some 40% — from nearly 2.19% in 1962–63 to an estimated 1.13% in 2004 to a projected 0.76% in the year 2025.[2]

In practical terms, many of us were worrying about a global population explosion at a time when the highest rate of growth in global population had already come and gone. The early projections of global population levels approaching 12 billion or even higher were simply way off the mark.

All of that is now ancient history. Looking forward, accounting for these decreases in rates of growth, the absolute level of global population is likely to level off sometime in the mid-century — probably at about 9.0 billion.[3] In fact, the United Nations, in a recently issued long-range forecast of population growth out to the year 2300, concluded that with the medium scenario the world population will stay in the nine-billion-person range.[4] Another estimate, from the International Institute for Applied Systems Analysis, suggests that the aggregate population level will peak in 2070 at about 9.0 billion persons and then begin a gradual decline.[5]

These latest projections are significantly different from many of the assumptions that have driven strategic planning decisions for decades. The revised projections suggest equally significant changes in the nature and growth of markets across the world. The fact is that our population is growing most quickly in those areas of the world least capable of supporting such growth, peaking in absolute numbers, continuing a 40-year decline in growth rate, and generating aging populations in what formerly were the most economically dynamic countries and regions of the world.

In the near future, Asia will remain the most populated area of the world. Currently, more than half the world's population lives in Asia; residents of China and India alone account for nearly two of every five people on the planet. In regional terms, the Near East — the Middle East and North Africa — will see the largest relative demographic increases, fueled by population booms across many countries — from Saudi Arabia to

Yemen, from Iran to Egypt. Sub-Saharan Africa will emerge as the world's fastest-growing region.[6]

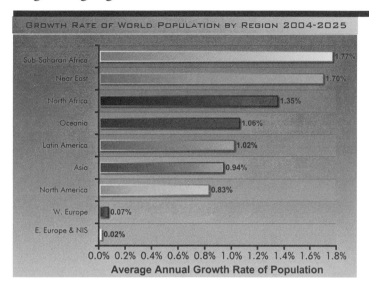

Another important dimension of this critical tectonic force — the third key element — is that we can expect to see significantly asymmetric rates of growth in regions and countries across the world. At the core of the continued absolute growth will be rapid population expansion in a number of developing countries. For example, many of the Least Developed Countries (LDCs), such as Nigeria and Zimbabwe, will experience extremely high rates of population growth. These countries are emblematic of the overall trend that the most rapid population growth is occurring in those regions and countries least capable of supporting such growth.

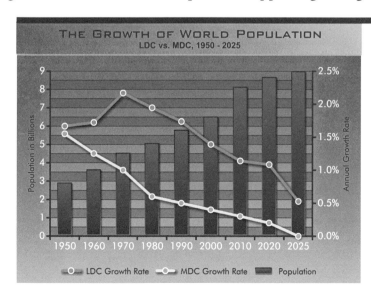

The prospect of booming populations in areas of the world marked previously by geopolitical instability suggests additional complications in the future. In particular, the question arises of how well economies will be able to soak up ever-larger labor segments emerging from their "youth

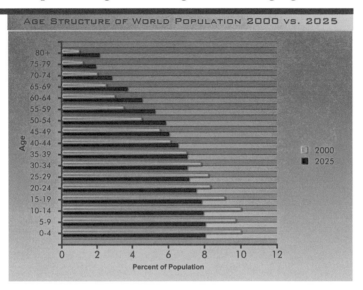

bulges." If economies fail to develop opportunities, the prospect of youth populations that become alienated and vulnerable to social, political, and religious radicalization certainly cannot be discounted.

These youth bulges can be expected to have a dual economic impact in Latin American, Sub-Saharan Africa, and Middle Eastern countries. In many of these states, large young populations will generate increased

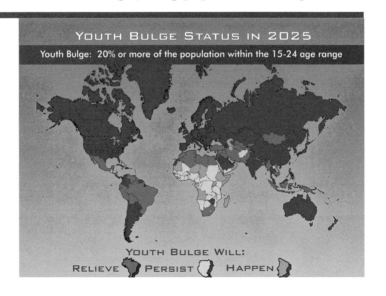

unemployment, resource scarcity, and enhanced demands for infrastructure, housing, education, and basic services. Increases in the relative size of the working population, though, will also attract labor-intensive industries and bolster economic growth. Many companies, such as Levi Strauss and Co. and General Electric, have already moved to India, China, and South America, where reduced labor costs bolster profitability. Some countries, such as India and China, have employed their vast pools of labor to reach higher levels of economic development.

In contrast to the rapid growth that we can anticipate in parts of the developing world, many developed countries will encounter stagnant population growth or even experience population contractions. In the former category — those countries that can expect stagnant growth — we can put the United States, which by virtue of its immigration inflows can look to avoid some of the more pronounced pressures affecting other developed economies. In the latter category, the situation in Japan, Western European states, and New Independent States (NISs) of the former Soviet Union will be profoundly different. To varying degrees, each of these countries faces the prospect of depopulation, as they shrink at an anticipated aggregate rate of some 350,000 people per year. Countries like Russia and Japan, if their current depopulations persist, could witness a decline on the order of one-third of their current populations out to the year 2050.[7]

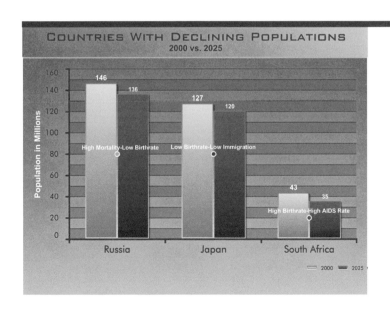

The upshot is that over the next 25 years, the developed countries as a group will drop in relative size, from an aggregate 20% of world population to around 15%.[8]   A decline this significant clearly has serious implications for business and economic trends in countries around the world. In the Organization for Economic Cooperation and Development (OECD) countries, declining populations and aging populations will put a high premium on advancements in health care, medical facilities, retirement facilities, and insurance — along with a host of other geriatric-specific services.

New migration and immigration patterns will undoubtedly emerge as a result of these shifting demographics. Rapid urbanization is accelerating in many developing countries. In China, for example, millions have left rural areas for the rapidly developing economic zones in urban centers such as Shanghai and Hong Kong. Managing these new population flows and the mega cities that result will strain the resources and services of LDCs as well as other countries.

In more than 50 countries, legal and illegal immigrants account for more than 15% of the population.[9] Immigration from countries where population growth fuels unemployment will likely increase. Current trends indicate, however, that the absorption rate of immigrants into developed economies will be lower than the population growth rate in developing countries of origin. This scenario will most likely result in the implementation of stricter immigration laws, more border patrols, and an increase in the number of illegal aliens. LDCs will also have to work to keep their best-educated and most productive workers from relocating to other countries, a process referred to as "brain drain."

Countries must weigh these negatives against the potential benefits of immigration, which can relieve problems created by a disproportionately large elderly population. The United States, for instance, has been able to maintain its proportionate share of the global population not through its own fertility level but rather through its open immigration policy. This same phenomenon applies in Canada, Australia, and New Zealand. Japan and many Western European countries will have to balance their strict immigration policies with their need to maintain a productive working-age population.

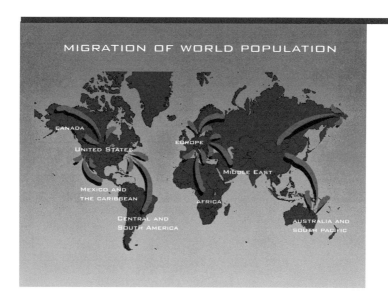

MIGRATION OF WORLD POPULATION

The next, and fourth, key dimension of this tectonic force is the graying of humanity. Our population is growing old and growing old quickly. By 2050, one of every five persons in the world will be at least 60 years old.[10] In Japan, the proportion of elderly people relative to the working population is already the highest in the world. Over the next 50 years, Japan's working-age population is expected to decline by more than 37 percent. By the year 2025, its ratio of elderly to productive workers is expected to fall to 1:2. Italy faces a similar decline, in both the collapse of its labor force and loss of productivity. Even in the United States, the aging of which will be tempered by immigration inflows, the population over the age of 65 will double to 70 million within 30 years. [11]

Aging populations across the world will present both challenges and opportunities for the public and private sectors. Declining birth rates and increasing longevity will increase costs in health care and pension funds, while at the same time reduce the size of the working population. As the labor pool ages, the burden of financing its retirement will fall on younger generations. There may also be a drop in national productivity, diminishing governments' abilities to provide services financed through current taxation rates. [12]

What will this tectonic force mean to business? First, these population trends will have a significant impact on the nature of economic activity, the rate of economic growth, the growth of markets, the demand for goods and services, the flows and volumes of capital, the availability of

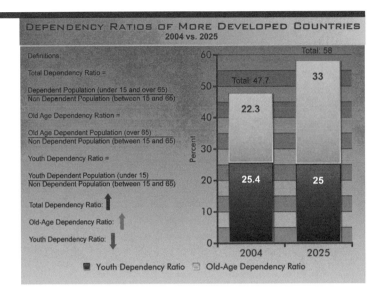

DEPENDENCY RATIOS OF MORE DEVELOPED COUNTRIES
2004 vs. 2025

Definitions:

Total Dependency Ratio =

Dependent Population (under 15 and over 65)
Non Dependent Population (between 15 and 65)

Old Age Dependency Ration =

Old Age Dependent Population (over 65)
Non Dependent Population (between 15 and 65)

Youth Dependency Ratio =

Youth Dependent Population (under 15)
Non Dependent Population (between 15 and 65)

Total Dependency Ratio:

Old-Age Dependency Ratio:

Youth Dependency Ratio:

■ Youth Dependency Ratio   ▢ Old-Age Dependency Ratio

labor, consumer tastes and preferences, and the use of natural resources and "strategic" resources, including food, water, and energy.

Second, these population trends translate into unprecedented require-ments for institutions across the board — from the largest governments to the most far-reaching corporations — to adapt to aging populations across the planet. Governments and corporations will need to adapt to aging labor pools, rising fiscal pressures from strained pension systems, rapidly changing consumer preferences aimed at ever-older age segments, and new lifestyles geared to the old, to name just a few of the changes this tectonic force implies.

Third, demographic trends will change the supply of labor and the demand for certain infrastructures and services. To gain competitive advantage, and to exploit the different market conditions now surfacing in various parts of the world, corporations must anticipate how countries will manage their age and youth bulges. Businesses should tailor their services and operations to these developing trends in urbanization and immigration.

Fourth, the prospect for new intergenerational frictions in many societies — especially those with a rapidly diminishing worker-to-retiree ratio — is significant. How will governments confront the difficult choice between sustaining welfare and pension systems that have been in place for decades and offering younger workers the same kind of lifestyles and social privileges that their parents have? Business could play a significant role in mediating these differences — by soaking up labor pools of older workers, deploying new technologies that enable higher productivity at older ages, and linking labor groups across countries.

Fifth, these trends all suggest that demographic change will have a significant impact on the broader geopolitical balance. For example, will spending on old age crowd out the capacities of governments, especially in Japan and Europe, to maintain strong capabilities in national defense and foreign policy? For that matter, what role will problematic fiscal decisions have on stifling government investment in research and development? The geopolitical outcome will affect the risk premiums that corporations attach to doing business in less stable parts of the world. It also could have implications for more systemic scenarios in which instability cuts into global output growth.

A quotation from an unknown person says: "Children are one-third of our population and all of our future." In light of this global tectonic, we need to think in broader terms. While children still are the bulk of our future, the intermediate reality is that longer lives, declining fertility, shifting social patterns, and wider stratification will all translate into a fundamentally different business environment across the planet.

URBANIZATION

CHAPTER
two

In the decades ahead, urbanization — the migration from rural to urban areas — will become a predominant global trend. Today, 47% of the world's population lives in an urban setting. By 2030, this proportion will rise to nearly 60%. [1]

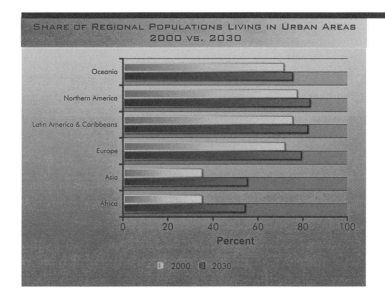

The implications of this population shift — this tectonic shift — from rural to urban in countries across the world are profound. It will create tremendous new pressures on federal and local governments, which will be faced with the challenge of providing physical infrastructure and social services to ever-expanding metropolitan populations. It will create new opportunities for business to satisfy a new set of requirements associated with rapidly growing urban centers. And it suggests the potential for unprecedented social, health-related, economic, and security volatility in the future.

The Least Developed Countries (LDCs) will see the most rapid and extreme urbanization. In 30 years, the urban population in LDCs will grow by approximately 2 billion people, resulting in metropolitan centers that cumulatively support more than 4 billion people. [2]

Looking forward, urbanization trends that once dominated Europe and the United States will characterize Asia — a continent already home to eight of the 15 largest cities in the world,[3] including Shanghai, Tokyo, Beijing, Mumbai, Calcutta, Jakarta, Delhi, and Osaka-Kobe. According

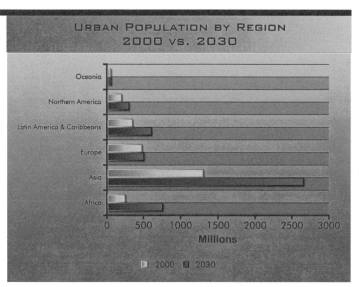

to the United Nations, each of these metropolises supports populations of 10 to 34 million inhabitants. By 2025, more than 50% of the total Asian population will reside in cities, an increase of 35% from current urban statistics.[4] China will have the largest urban population in the world, with nearly 827 million people. India will have the second largest, with 586 million people.

Megacities — metropolitan areas that support more than 10 million inhabitants — will be a key by-product of urbanization. Cities such as Jakarta and Mumbai will become a feature of Asian urbanization as they join the ranks of New York, Shanghai, and Tokyo, currently the world's largest metropolitan areas. By 2015, Asia will have 18 megacities, Latin America will have four, and North America will have two.[5] Europe will not have an urban center of this magnitude. Tokyo, now the largest city in the world with a population of approximately 28.7 million inhabitants, will be rivaled in size by Mumbai, with a projected population of 27.4 million people. Lagos will have an estimated future population of 24.4 million people.

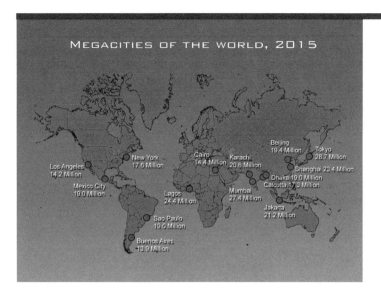

MEGACITIES OF THE WORLD, 2015

Beijing 19.4 Million
Tokyo 28.7 Million
New York 17.6 Million
Cairo 14.4 Million
Karachi 20.6 Million
Shanghai 23.4 Million
Los Angeles 14.2 Million
Dhaka 19.0 Million
Calcutta 17.3 Million
Mexico City 19.0 Million
Lagos 24.4 Million
Mumbai 27.4 Million
Jakarta 21.2 Million
Sao Paulo 19.0 Million
Buenos Aires 13.9 Million

Rapid urbanization carries with it new challenges associated with rural development. Rural communities will languish as their populations diminish, and governments will likely attempt to develop their country-side to slow emigration to the cities. Projects providing rural areas with electricity, potable water, better roads, new transportation facilities, and employment incentives could improve living conditions and slow the demographic shift from country to city.

What are the implications of urbanization for business? The first area of opportunity will flow from the renewal and modernization requirements of megacities. The exigencies of size and population density in large urban centers will allow business to play an enhanced role in innovation, investment, and economic growth. Transportation shortcomings, improper allocation of resources, housing shortages, waste control, extensive air and water pollution, and city congestion will all take their toll on the quality of life in cities. Second, business has an opportunity to work with governments in rural development, which could serve to alleviate the burdens brought on by the rise of megacities.

DISEASE AND GLOBALIZATION

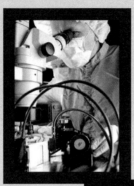

CHAPTER
three

In this era of globalization, infectious disease thrives along with cross-border integration — including the movement of goods, labor, and transportation. The international community already contends with viruses such as HIV, malaria, SARS, and tuberculosis. It must contend with this downside of globalization in the context of accelerating population growth, urbanization, and international integration.

The stakes associated with this tectonic force are high. Infectious diseases kill millions of people every year and, as the SARS virus demonstrated, can quickly generate economic turmoil on a global scale.

As populations continue to interconnect, the likelihood of epidemics and pandemics of infectious disease increases. SARS, for example, originated in China and spread rapidly to 30 countries — with more severe outbreaks in Toronto, Taiwan, and Beijing. As global health organizations, in particular the World Health Organization, struggled to identify and contain the virus, SARS grounded airlines, hurt businesses, and even caused riots in China.[1] The global economic impact of SARS was estimated at $30 billion, with an estimated $12.3 billion in losses in Asia alone.[2]

Because trade and travel now link so many societies, SARS-like epidemics and their human and economic consequences can no longer come as a surprise. Businesses must be able to adapt quickly to changed market conditions brought about by such epidemics.

The ability of infectious diseases to spread in a more integrated world is well documented. The 1997 outbreak of cholera in Peru, infecting nearly 10,000 people, occurred when a Japanese ship carrying export goods emptied its infected bilge waste into the Peruvian water system.[3] In other examples, the dengue fever and West Nile viruses recently appeared in the United States, and African prairie dogs, exported to the United States in 2003 as pets, caused a monkey pox outbreak in the Midwest. [4]

Infectious disease significantly impacts economic growth and development, especially in countries with high disease burdens.[5] In many developing countries, HIV/AIDS has decimated the labor force and overwhelmed already-struggling education and health care systems. The catastrophic social and economic effects will affect those countries for generations to come.

It is important to note that those countries with the most underdeveloped public health services record the highest infection rates. Of the 42 million

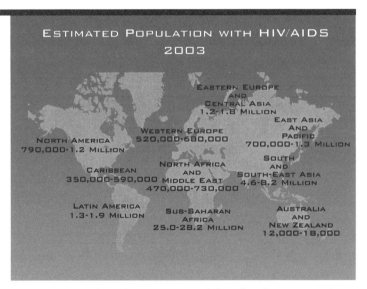

people now diagnosed with AIDS worldwide, for example, 95% live in the developing world — with Africa reporting the majority of new cases.[6] In sub-Saharan Africa, currently the worst-affected region of the world, 25–28 million people live with AIDS.[7] By 2010, however, this region will no longer rank as the most HIV-infected region; China, Ethiopia, India, Nigeria, and Russia will become the new centers of the AIDS epidemic. Cumulatively, these states are trying to support between 14 and 23 million people living with AIDS, numbers that will increase to 75 million people by 2010.[8] These infection rates will reduce productivity, GDP, and foreign direct investment. Today, the AIDS epidemic rages in many developing countries that must also contend with malaria, yellow fever, and dengue fever. Together, these diseases

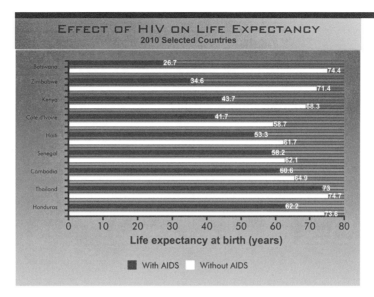

EFFECT OF HIV ON LIFE EXPECTANCY
2010 Selected Countries

Life expectancy at birth (years)

Botswana: 26.7, 74.4
Zimbabwe: 34.6, 71.4
Kenya: 43.7, 68.3
Cote d'Ivoire: 41.7, 58.7
Haiti: 53.3, 61.7
Senegal: 58.2, 62.1
Cambodia: 60.6, 64.9
Thailand: 73, 74.7
Honduras: 62.2, 73.6

■ With AIDS □ Without AIDS

have already orphaned millions of children, discouraged foreign investment, and impaired the health care infrastructure.

As we look into the future, the threat of biological terrorism must also be taken into account as a key potential force in shaping the business — and overall — environment. This new threat makes the issue of disease proliferation all the more significant.

Smallpox is a case in point. Because many countries stopped their small-pox vaccination programs in the 1970s, a biological attack with this potential terrorist weapon would create a humanitarian disaster.[9] In light of this threat, Israel and the United States recently vaccinated their mili-tary personnel. Following the terrorist attacks of September 11, 2001, and the subsequent release of anthrax through the U.S. postal system, many countries now work to prevent terrorist groups from gaining access to dangerous bio-agents. Infectious disease has become an issue of national and international security for the entire global community.

Countries need a global health infrastructure that responds quickly and effectively to epidemics such as SARS or to terrorist-induced disease out-breaks. In this era of increased economic and social integration, an out-break in one country can develop into a global pandemic in a matter of days. As a result, governments, nongovernment organizations (NGOs), and private companies must devise health care solutions that cross bor-ders as effectively as the infectious agents they work to contain.

International disease control will present vast opportunities and challenges to businesses operating in afflicted countries or working to provide containment products and services. The ability of these corporations, along with governments and NGOs, to react and respond to outbreaks, and to devise solutions that meet the health care needs of the world's population, will be critical to continued global prosperity.

More specifically, what should businesses be doing to prepare for contingencies arising from natural or deliberate epidemics and disease-related volatility? First, they need to engage in scenario-analysis in order to begin to define their reactions in the event of an epidemic. Second, they should assess the extent to which international and national institutions are prepared for such contingencies — especially because public–private sector partnership is critical to defining and implementing solutions. Finally, the growing threat of bioterrorism suggests new possibilities for the private sector to marshal its resources and technological innovation in support of new biodefenses and procedures.

RESOURCE
MANAGEMENT

CHAPTER
four

Businesses around the world must remain attentive to changes in the availability of critical resources—water, food, and energy. Maintaining productive labor forces and viable corporate operations depends on these inputs, the accessibility of which varies with population growth and technological advancement.

Over the next 25 years, businesses will play a key role in inventing and developing new technologies such as desalinization plants, biotechnology, and renewable fuels to help relieve resource scarcity. Corporations and governments will partner to improve food production and distribution, water system management, and energy efficiency in many countries currently facing shortages.

A critical resource, monitored closely, is fresh water. The reality is that only one-half of 1 percent of the vast amount of water that covers the Earth's surface is available for human consumption.[1] The abundant renewable freshwater sources in North and South America and Australia

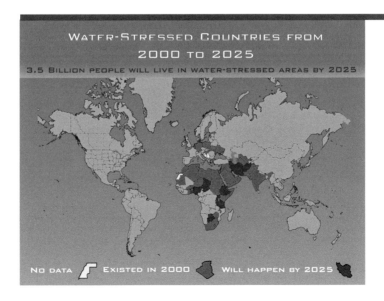

will not decline significantly in the years to come, but more than 1 billion people now living in sub-Saharan Africa, the Middle East, and India already face a serious scarcity of potable water. These shortages result from a natural lack of renewable freshwater sources and the large role of irrigation in agriculture. If current trends in population growth and water demand persist, these areas will face severe water shortages in the near future.

Conflict over water resources is possible in several distinct regions, but it is most pronounced in the Middle East. [2] In Israel, water for agriculture is used efficiently but not sustainably. Furthermore, Palestinian territories lack sufficient drinking water for their dense populations. Israel and Lebanon have exchanged hostilities over Lebanon's construction of a pumping station upriver from Israel. Turkey created serious frictions with the Syrian government with its construction of more than a dozen dams along the Tigris and Euphrates — upriver from Syria.

To solve and avoid similar disputes in other international riparian zones, affected countries need to employ measures that encourage technological innovation and cooperation. Beyond that, world leaders have to develop cost-effective measures to increase fresh water availability and control demand. They must also work to preserve water supplies through more efficient irrigation techniques, dams, and pipelines. Some Middle Eastern and North African countries are already constructing desalination plants. Despite protests, water-stressed governments in India and Mexico have invited corporations to privatize freshwater allocation to consumers. These cases suggest that as water scarcity increases, businesses will take the lead researching and implementing new water management processes, facilities, and technologies.

The availability of food, the second resource under consideration, is tied to population growth, governance, and technology. In crisis countries, a combination of low agricultural productivity, drought, poor distribution systems, population growth, and political unrest have all increased the demand for food aid. Such circumstances require donor nations to elevate production and employ more efficient distribution systems.

In the near future, a combination of technology and increased market efficiency could serve to help alleviate food crises around the world.

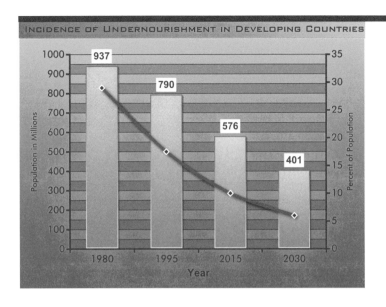

INCIDENCE OF UNDERNOURISHMENT IN DEVELOPING COUNTRIES

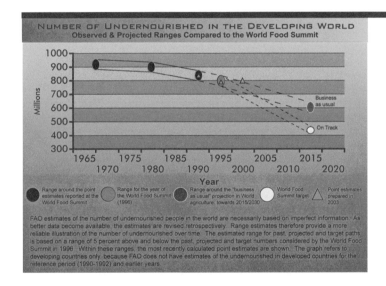

NUMBER OF UNDERNOURISHED IN THE DEVELOPING WORLD
Observed & Projected Ranges Compared to the World Food Summit

Companies have already boosted crop yields of a variety of food staples by engineering plants resistant to pests, droughts, and diseases. Scientists have also modified and supplemented common foods, such as rice, to include essential vitamins.

Many believe that agricultural productivity in food aid countries will increase when agricultural trade barriers are reduced, especially in the United States and the European Union, in the context of the Doha Round of the World Trade Organization.

Developing countries contend that farm subsidies in wealthier countries exacerbate food shortages and increase their dependency on assistance. Finally, political instability has also been a root cause of famine in a number of developing countries — most recently in Zimbabwe. Mitigating the disruption of supply lines and the politicization of food aid will certainly improve nutrition in a number of crisis countries.

Energy availability is an ongoing and conventional business concern. The central question surrounding the management of fuel resources is not whether fossil fuels will continue to dominate the market, but whether alternative, renewable sources of energy will gain widespread acceptance. Power provided by fossil fuel sources is cheaply extracted, but

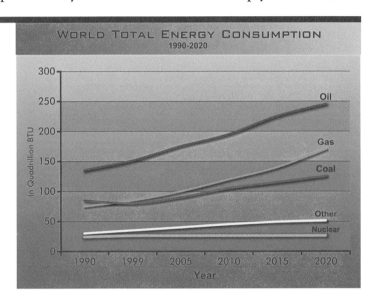

environmentally destructive. Some renewable, environmentally friendly energy sources — such as solar, hydro, and wind — have been implemented, but their market price remains significantly higher than conventional gas, oil, and coal energy resources. Without any serious incentives to overturn the energy status quo, most industries will continue to rely on oil and gas, much of which come from deep reserves in the Middle East.

Despite significant reserves in fossil fuels, companies and governments may still struggle to meet the energy demands of growing urban populations. In the summer of 2003, blackouts hit five U.S. cities, including New York City. Separate power outages also affected major cities in

Eastern Canada, Britain, and Denmark. Losing electricity in these urban areas revealed the effects of aging energy networks, coupled with rising demand. Given the economic losses suffered during these power failures, governments will likely begin remodeling their energy infrastructure and investigating market-based solutions to energy shortages.[3]

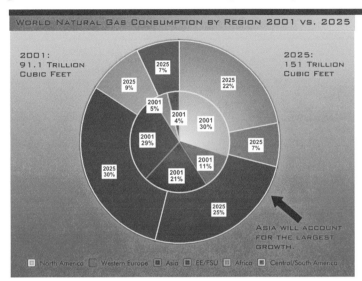

WORLD NATURAL GAS CONSUMPTION BY REGION 2001 vs. 2025

2001: 91.1 TRILLION CUBIC FEET

2025: 151 TRILLION CUBIC FEET

ASIA WILL ACCOUNT FOR THE LARGEST GROWTH.

North America   Western Europe   Asia   EE/FSU   Africa   Central/South America

In the future, the regulation and availability of food, water, and energy will present many challenges and opportunities to businesses around the world. Good governance will make all resources more accessible, while advances in technology will help alleviate food and water shortages. Fossil fuels will be available at relatively low costs, and it is possible—perhaps even probable — that technological and political change will lead to increased reliance on alternative energy sources. Business and community leaders should pay careful attention to trends in the availability of water, food, and energy to manage their resources more efficiently for the future.

Necessarily, businesses are invested in the way in which this tectonic force of strategic resources unfolds in the years ahead. The stability and security of the broader macroeconomic environment will depend on the success with which countries across the world can provide food and water to relentlessly expanding populations. The viability of commercial operations across the globe will depend on energy intensity, the price and efficiency of energy supplies, and the stability of energy supplies and prices. And technological innovation propelled by the private sector will play an extremely important role in the degree to which humanity can improve its stewardship of food, water, and energy.

ENVIRONMENTAL
DEGRADATION

CHAPTER
five

During the 1992 United Nations Conference on the Environment, world leaders committed themselves and their countries to the principle of sustainable development—economic and social development that would ensure future generations a healthy and productive life in harmony with nature.[1] In its 1992 World Development Report, the World Bank clarified the relationship between development and the environment, noting that a country's environmental problems often corresponded to its level of economic development.[2] It has since become apparent that many Least Developed Countries (LDCs) suffer from erosion, desertification, biodiversity loss, and deforestation, while more-developed industrialized countries contend mostly with air and water pollution associated with manufacturing, fossil fuel use, and land conversion. Clearly, the industrialization of developing economies, combined with sustained growth in developed countries, will exacerbate worldwide environmental degradation.

A global pursuit of stronger environmental protection and health standards intended to prevent this trend would increase regulatory and other costs for businesses. On the other hand, higher standards would stimulate investment in more environmentally sound manufacturing and production technologies.

Concerned with the environmental and health effects of pollution, businesses, governments, and NGOs have debated a range of possible policy responses to environmental degradation. Global warming, caused by fossil fuel conversion and the subsequent release of greenhouse gases (GHGs) into the atmosphere, has moved to the forefront of international discussions. In 1997, world leaders looking for means to curb fossil-fuel use created the Kyoto Protocol. Signatories to the treaty hoped it would limit pollution while correcting inequities in the production of GHGs.[3] Presently, North America, a region with 5% of the world's population,

produces more than 40% of all manmade carbon dioxide.[4] This trend
will change in the near future, though, as countries with much larger
populations — including India, China, and Brazil — continue to indus-
trialize and assume a larger share of global emissions.

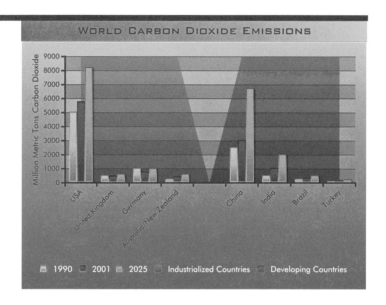

Although the Kyoto Protocol will not enter into force, it serves as a sign
that reliance on oil and gas as the primary fuels for economic growth and
development will continue to come into question in the future.   Any
international, regional, or domestic plan to limit fossil-fuel conversion in
an effort to reduce GHG emissions would have considerable implications

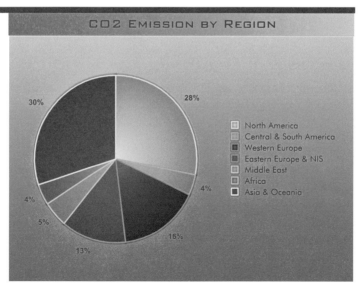

environmental degradation

for businesses worldwide. Policies such as a carbon tax or a carbon cap and trade system, outlined in Kyoto and other pollution control treaties, would fundamentally alter the way business is conducted.

Governments are also initiating plans to reduce air and water concentrations of sulfur dioxide, mercury, arsenic, and nitrogen oxide, compounds emitted mainly from coal power plants and manufacturing facilities. Many policymakers believe market-based solutions that specify a limited number of permits to pollute, bought and sold at market price, will be the most efficient method of reaching higher levels of environmental protection. Given this policy's popularity in Europe and its use in the U.S. Clear Skies Plan, corporations should now consider how to remain competitive in the face of tighter regulations enforced through "cap and trade" systems.[5]

Environmental policymakers must also contend with water pollution. In 1998, The United Nations Education, Scientific, and Cultural Organization (UNESCO) labeled 40% of U.S. water bodies as unfit for recreational use because of nutrient, metal, and agricultural pollution. Only five of 55 European rivers were designated pristine. In Asia, all rivers traversing major cities were characterized as severely polluted. [6]

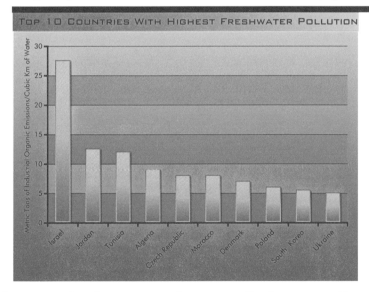

The links between development and water pollution are well established. Industry adds approximately 300–500 million tons of heavy metals, solvents, and toxic sludge to the water system each year. Developing countries dump 70% of their untreated industrial waste into their waters, further polluting the usable water supply. [7]

Industrial water use rises with country income, increasing from 10% of total water use for low- and middle-income countries, to approximately 59% for high-income countries. Projected estimates indicate that the annual volume of water consumed by industry will rise from 752 cubic kilometers per year in 1995 to an estimated 1,170 cubic kilometers per year in 2025.[8]

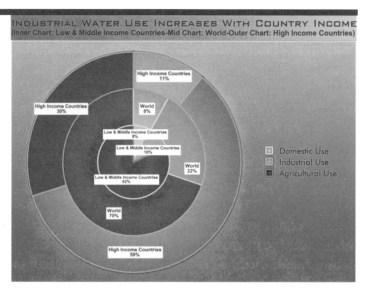

INDUSTRIAL WATER USE INCREASES WITH COUNTRY INCOME
(Inner Chart: Low & Middle Income Countries-Mid Chart: World-Outer Chart: High Income Countries)

High Income Countries 11%
High Income Countries 30%
World 8%
Low & Middle Income Countries 8%
Low & Middle Income Countries 10%
World 22%
Low & Middle Income Countries 82%
World 70%
High Income Countries 59%

Domestic Use
Industrial Use
Agricultural Use

Although industry alone does not account for all water pollution, current trends of increasing corporate water use and pollution cannot continue unabated. Given the scarcity of fresh water available for drinking and recreation, businesses will face tougher measures aimed at conserving and protecting existing water supplies.

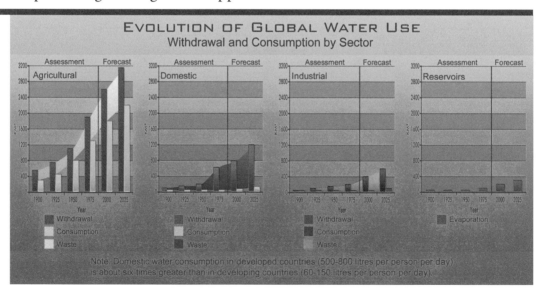

EVOLUTION OF GLOBAL WATER USE
Withdrawal and Consumption by Sector

Note: Domestic water consumption in developed countries (500-800 litres per person per day) is about six times greater than in developing countries (60-150 litres per person per day).

environmental degradation

Rising public concern over environmental pollution has generated greater corporate investment in the research and development of environmentally sound products. A number of auto manufacturers, notably Honda and Toyota, have begun testing fuel-efficient and fuel cell cars on U.S. roads.[9] Shell Corporation (Showa Shell) has partnered with the Iwatani Corporation to open the first liquid hydrogen refueling station in Tokyo.[10] Countries around the world are also exploring methods of creating and conserving energy and water.

These examples of leading global corporations preparing for the future indicate the importance attached to environmental policy by the business community. Given public concern over air and water pollution, companies that want to maintain an edge in their industry should follow environmental trends carefully.

Increased industrialization, commercial agricultural development, and urbanization also raise the conservation issues of deforestation and biodiversity loss. For LDCs that lack the resources to develop and enforce environmental protection laws, these problems are more serious. The Food and Agriculture Organization (FAO) estimated that 53,000 square miles of tropical forests, mostly in South America, were felled annually throughout the 1980s. Southeast Asia (Cambodia, Indonesia, Laos, Malaysia, Myanmar, Thailand, and Vietnam) lost nearly as much forest per year as the Brazilian Amazon from the mid-1970s to the mid-1980s, with 4,800 square miles per year converted to agriculture or cut for timber.[11]

Governments of some developing countries are now working to combine property rights and capitalism to help prevent environmental degradation while also promoting business development. For example, countries such as Mexico and Costa Rica have invited pharmaceutical and cosmetic corporations to mine biodiversity within their borders. The corporations hope to find new medicines, perfumes, and cosmetic products, while the host countries believe "bio-mining" may allow corporate development to augment biodiversity conservation.

Desertification and erosion, as well as pollution and deforestation, pose additional threats to environmental protection around the world. The gradual loss of soil productivity, resulting from land overuse, forest fires, excessive fertilizer use, and overgrazing, has become a worldwide problem directly affecting dryland ecosystems, which make up a third of the Earth's land surface (more than 4 billion hectares).

Secretary General of the United Nations Kofi Annan notes that, "Current estimates are that the livelihoods of more than 1 billion people are at risk from desertification, and that, as a consequence, 135 million people may be in danger of being driven from their land".[12] Desertification affects two-thirds of Africa, more than one-third of the United States, and one-quarter of Latin America. In China, expanding deserts have taken nearly 700,000 hectares of cultivated land, 2.35 million hectares of rangeland, and 6.4 million hectares of forests, woodlands, and shrub lands. Worldwide, approximately 70% of the 5.2 billion hectares of dry lands used for agriculture are already degraded.[13]

These soil-loss problems threaten agriculture, husbandry, and water systems on every continent except Antarctica. Governments, multilateral institutions, NGOs, and private corporations now partner to address the issues through poverty relief, the instituting of property rights, and technology transfers. Many countries facing desertification will rely on corporations to develop drought-tolerant plants, better irrigation processes, and new approaches to agriculture and husbandry.

Though the international community must contend with a myriad of environmental problems, pollution, biodiversity loss, and desertification will prove to be the most challenging. Regulatory responses to these environmental issues will have a far-reaching and extensive impact on businesses. At the same time, policymakers must recognize that environmental protection has historically been most successful when industry agrees and complies with conservation policies. Concerted efforts between businesses and governments can result in policies beneficial to environmental protection and corporate viability.

SECTION TWO

Commerce
and
Knowledge

ECONOMIC INTEGRATION

CHAPTER
six

The driving forces behind globalization — including faster communication, improved transportation, increased flows of goods and services, labor mobility, the proliferation of technology, and ever more rapid financial flows — have profoundly affected the world's economic landscape. Increased cross-border economic activity, specifically in the form of trade and investment, has contributed significantly to the overall growth of the global economy to approximately $47 trillion — or about four times its corresponding level in the mid-1970s.[1]

The increase in the movement of cross-border factor endowments — trade in goods and services, labor, capital, technology, knowledge, and other factors — has grown faster than the pace of aggregate output. We can expect this trend to continue, as the logic of comparative advantage and efforts to reduce tariff and nontariff barriers offer the possibility of even higher efficiencies brought about by trade.

Access to international markets has proven essential to the economic growth and development of middle-income economies such as China, India, South Korea, and Taiwan. These new economies now have assumed a key role in world trade sectors as diverse as high-technology manufacturing and textiles. Clearly, in today's integrated global economy, neither countries nor companies can afford to operate in isolation. Corporations, therefore, should anticipate the continued globalization of production and consumption and formulate their strategies accordingly.

The Airbus Consortium offers a telling example of how corporations conduct business across a much more highly integrated global economic system. Britain exports the aircraft's wings, while Germany supplies the fuselage and the tail. Spain manufactures the doors, and France oversees cockpit production and final assembly. More than 800 American companies supply in excess of 35% of the Consortium's aircraft components, with

1,500 other providers located in approximately 30 additional countries. Airbus employs some 48,000 people, representing more than 50 nationalities, and is now one of the many corporations that contract foreign companies to manufacture products that are then sold around the world.[2]

The Airbus example is representative of a bigger global picture — a picture in which the largest and most prosperous economies are the most fully integrated. Dominant players, like those economies involved in Airbus, are located in Western Europe, the United States, and Japan. Collectively, these regions account for the lion's share of global output as well as global trade and investment.[3]

A number of middle-income economies have engineered rapid development paths in large part because of the internationalization of their economies. This is another key feature of the integrated economy around us. Countries with high levels of foreign direct investment (FDI) and other cross-border integration, such as Singapore, have become the economic success stories of recent decades.[4] As these states have opened their borders to trade and investment, corporations have capitalized on new possibilities and expanded existing market opportunities.

Multinational corporations (MNCs) have been a powerful catalyst in the process of cross-border integration. In some cases, companies have grown more powerful financially than some of the countries in which they operate. Of the 100 largest economies in the world, 51 are global corporations and 49 are countries.[5]

ECONOMIC ENTITIES TOP 30
OF THE WORLD'S LARGEST ECONOMIC ENTITIES, 51 ARE CORPORATIONS AND 49 ARE COUNTRIES

RANK	COUNTRY/CORPORATION	GDP/SALES ($ MM)	RANK	COUNTRY/CORPORATION	GDP/SALES ($ MM)
1	UNITED STATES	8,708,870	16	RUSSIAN FED.	375,345
2	JAPAN	4,395,083	17	ARGENTINA	281,942
3	GERMANY	2,081,202	18	SWITZERLAND	260,299
4	FRANCE	1,410,262	19	BELGIUM	245,706
5	UNITED KINGDOM	1,373,612	20	SWEDEN	226,388
6	ITALY	1,149,958	21	AUSTRIA	208,949
7	CHINA	1,149,814	22	TURKEY	188,374
8	BRAZIL	760,345	23	GENERAL MOTORS	176,558
9	CANADA	612,049	24	DENMARK	174,363
10	SPAIN	562,245	25	WAL-MART	166,809
11	MEXICO	474,951	26	EXXON MOBIL	163,881
12	INDIA	459,765	27	FORD MOTOR	162,558
13	KOREA, REP.	406,940	28	DAIMLERCHRYSLER	159,985
14	AUSTRALIA	389,691	29	POLAND	154,146
15	NETHERLANDS	384,766	30	NORWAY	145,449

Conversely, the data suggest that poorer countries are less likely to be linked to global markets or attract FDI. Sub-Saharan and North African countries attract the lowest levels of FDI; therefore, it comes as little surprise that many countries in these regions have recorded negative economic growth and declining GDP per capita. Investment flows have been directed to middle-income developing countries, such as Mexico and China, with higher levels of economic dynamism and more attractive investment environments.[6]

There is no straightforward explanation for why some economies have successfully integrated into the world trading system and others have economically languished.

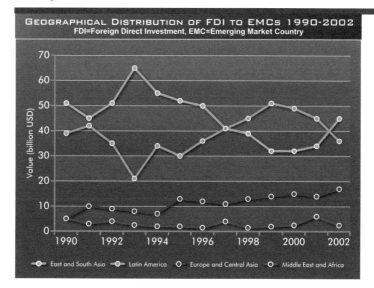

Economists agree that no one solution assures growth and development, but countries can implement certain practices to attract FDI and bolster both development and national output. In general, countries that demonstrate certain general economic, political, and social characteristics are able to command greater levels of world trade and capital flows.

Factors in economic, political, and social stability:[7]
- Rule enforcement, regarding operations standards, and treatment of foreign affiliates;
- Policies on the structure of markets (especially competition and M&A policies);
- International trade and investment agreements;
- Privatization policy;

- Trade policy (tariffs and nontariff barriers) and coherence
  of FDI and trade policies;
- Favorable tax policy;
- Low levels of corruption.

Though foreign affiliates may invest for a variety of other reasons, such as the availability of cheap labor or raw resources, these principles remain fundamental to corporate risk analysis. Many of the poorest countries do not meet these standard investment criteria and as a result are unable to accumulate financial or physical capital. For example, the Democratic Republic of Congo is a country where civil unrest, disease, and poor infrastructure make it dangerous for foreign investors. Though the country can attract firms interested in diamond and gold mining, the extraction of raw resources, coupled with lack of investment in labor and severe corruption, has undermined economic growth and country development. Generally speaking, states such as the Democratic Republic of Congo are consumed by domestic problems that prevent them from integrating with world markets.[8]

Though economic integration is an imperfect process, the financial links between countries will grow stronger in the future. Since the 1994 Uruguay Round of World Trade Organization (WTO) negotiations, developing countries have pined for greater access to agriculture and textile markets. Similarly, developed countries have tried to advance agreements on the protection of investment and intellectual property.[9] Given the slow and contentious nature of WTO negotiations — the 2003 Cancún talks, for example, broke down over agricultural protectionism — many countries choose not to wait for multilateral resolutions.[10] Instead, many negotiate and enter into bilateral and regional trade agreements. The North American Free Trade Agreement (NAFTA), for instance, is one of an almost countless array of agreements connecting countries in what is now referred to as the "spaghetti bowl effect."[11] Though debate continues over whether regional agreements promote or hinder multilateral free trade, it is likely that countries will continue negotiating for greater market access in both regional and global trade forums.

Based on current trends, integration into the global economic system will remain a top priority for corporate and country leaders. Companies with assets abroad must closely monitor the economic vitality of their foreign affiliates. Exchange rate and financial crisis are direct results of capital market integration, and firms must carefully track country indicators for signs of financial weakness. This will not be easy for commercial players like the Airbus Consortium that maintain operations around the globe.

In order to respond to this global tectonic of economic integration, corporations will have to devise a constellation of new management strategies to track political developments and monitor the productivity of thousands of employees in numerous countries. Despite the risks associated with global integration, over the last 30 years the benefits of free trade, open capital markets, and international expansion have far outweighed the costs. Companies should anticipate and prepare for the continued integration of financial and goods markets, as well as the development of stronger economic ties among countries across the planet.

KNOWLEDGE DISSEMINATION

CHAPTER
seven

Knowledge, the production and dissemination of context-dependent information, plays an increasingly important role in wealth generation around the world. In this Third Wave economy, ideas and know-how are proving to be as valuable as the traditional factors of production: capital, land, and labor. In developed countries, knowledge-based industries such as telecommunications and software will continue to grow,[1] forcing older industries such as steel and automotive to shift production overseas to take advantage of cheaper materials and labor. By 2012, it is projected that the U.S. manufacturing sector will lose 200,000 jobs.[2] The knowledge economy will place demands on businesses to seek new windows of opportunity, maintain an educated workforce, and invest in research and development.

Collecting and redistributing information, a way to leverage knowledge among industries, has increased business efficiency, enabling companies to make more informed decisions. Information sharing has helped end the duplication of effort, saving time and resources. Most organizations now prefer to share information with their stakeholders, clients, and suppliers through the Internet, helping them improve their overall business strategies and product offerings. The speed of knowledge dissemination has resulted in shorter product development cycles and increased overall IT capability and capacity, with corresponding declines in the cost of hardware and transmission.

World leaders have responded to the rise of the knowledge economy by emphasizing educational development to attract or maintain business investment. A December 2002 World Bank report warns that developing countries will need to close the knowledge gap, even though many of these states lack the educational systems and technological infrastructure to be competitive in a knowledge-based economy. [3]

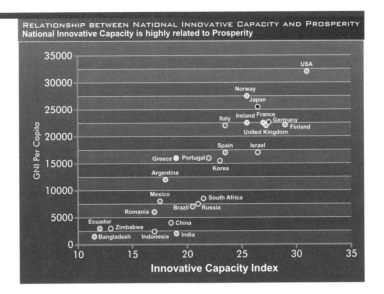

RELATIONSHIP BETWEEN NATIONAL INNOVATIVE CAPACITY AND PROSPERITY
National Innovative Capacity is highly related to Prosperity

These developing countries will need to increase investments in higher education institutions and encourage advancements in tertiary education, with the goal of increasing the availability of skilled labor and productivity.[4] Business leaders interested in hiring a well-educated workforce will begin to view these countries and their less costly, skilled workforce as critical resources.

The trend in education is already visible, with Asian students in Asian universities earning more than 1.1 million of the 2.6 million science and engineering bachelor's degrees conferred across the world in 2000.

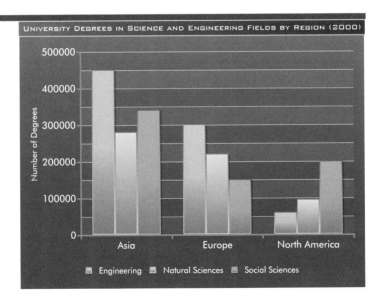

UNIVERSITY DEGREES IN SCIENCE AND ENGINEERING FIELDS BY REGION (2000)

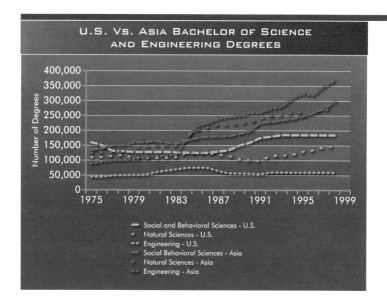

The United States — traditionally the world leader in higher education — is now among ten countries that provide a college education to approximately one-third or more of its college-age population.[5] The rest of the world is catching up quickly.

Governments and corporations are just beginning to learn how to manage and protect knowledge- or technology-based economies. Businesses that facilitate the creation of new technologies find that patents on information are difficult to obtain on the international level.

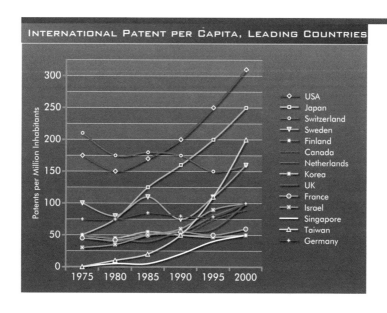

Piracy and counterfeiting are also critical issues. The problem of piracy, for instance, is highly visible in the recording industry. Internet-created file-sharing programs for use by anyone have resulted in the loss of millions of dollars of potential record/CD sales. Worldwide CD and DVD replication rose to 11.7 billion units in 2004.[6] The pirated music market, based only on the prices of pirated products sold, was estimated at $4.6 billion in 2002.[7] Part of the explanation is a lack of institutional capacity. Technology and economic transformation are outpacing international legal institutions, and governments must work with corporations to establish more functional mechanisms for safeguarding investment in intellectual property.

Cyberterrorism poses an additional threat to corporations and industries running online operations in the growing knowledge economy. Just one attack by a hacker or computer virus can cause several million dollars of damage. The worm, "SoBig," infected nearly half a million computers worldwide, overwhelming mail servers with excess false messages. The bug also disrupted Amtrak train schedules and hurt Air Canada's systems, while hampering government offices and universities trying to stop the virus.[8] In the future, fighting worms and bugs will require heavier investment. Software producers will have to develop more protective codes, and service providers will need to anticipate attacks and devise contingency plans to counter potential damage.

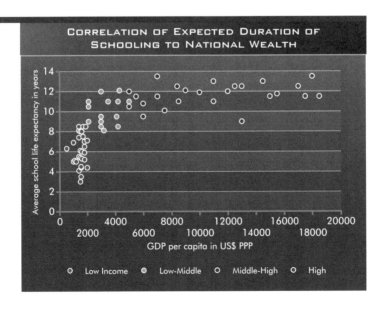

Though it poses a new set of business challenges, knowledge is now a necessary ingredient in the recipe for economic development. Businesses looking to remain competitive must be cognizant of how this Third Wave economy is taking hold around the world. Current trends indicate that manufacturers of raw materials will relocate to countries with uneducated workforces, with abundant and inexpensive labor. Similarly, corporations that rely on skilled labor will also invest where the workforce is least expensive, but still possesses the training and skills necessary to facilitate production.

Corporations must, therefore, take advantage of the opportunities presented by the rise of education and dissemination of technological know-how around the world. Business managers should anticipate how the knowledge economy would change business operations throughout the next 20 years and beyond.

SECTION THREE

Technology and Change

INFORMATION
TECHNOLOGY

CHAPTER
eight

In recent decades, Information Technology (IT) has fundamentally changed how people live, work, learn, and interact with one another. This major tectonic force will shape business, society, politics, and the environment well into the future.

As IT continues to develop as an industry, the resulting technological advancements will make communication, information flow, and business transactions faster, more accurate, and less expensive. Like every successful technology, IT-derived products and technologies will become more efficient and less costly, and maintain worldwide demand.

Growth in IT has enhanced economic development worldwide. Economies such as Hong Kong, Singapore, and Taiwan have benefited tremendously from the manufacture and sale of IT products.

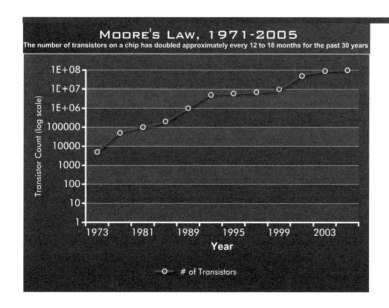

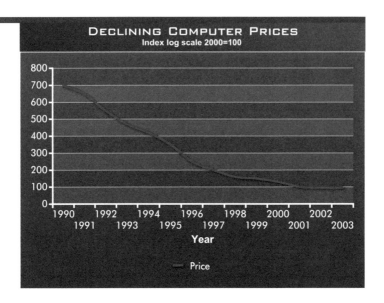

DECLINING COMPUTER PRICES
Index log scale 2000=100

— Price

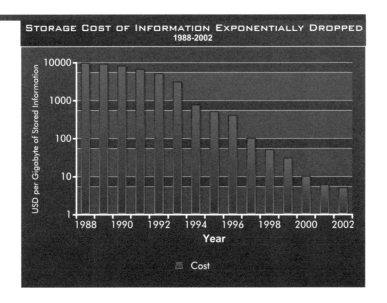

STORAGE COST OF INFORMATION EXPONENTIALLY DROPPED
1988-2002

USD per Gigabyte of Stored Information

Year

▨ Cost

For all countries, technology has increased the speed of business transactions and information flows, effectively making the world a much smaller place. By 2015, India will remain in the forefront of IT development and China will lead the world in IT utilization. The impact will go well beyond China and India, as important as those countries will be. Latin America's Internet market will grow exponentially as countries deregulate their telecom industries, pursue developing IT markets, and adopt new technologies.[1] Countries such as Argentina, Mexico, and Brazil will present investors with vast opportunities in the telecom industry. The rapid expansion of these information and knowledge flows also has an important social dimension. The continued spread of IT will enhance cultural and business exchange in a way that will open traditionally closed societies, such as China and Saudi Arabia.

IT will be an ever more vital and multidimensional part of our daily lives — supporting our activities at home, work, and school. Although Internet access varies by income, education, race, age, and location, overall access has increased across all of these groups. The share of U.S. households with Internet access increased from 26.2% in December 1998 to 41.5% in August 2000, and to more than 60% by 2003. In 2003, the market was estimated at $6.9 billion. During the same period, the share of individuals using the Internet rose from 32.7% to 44.4%, and today exceeds 60%.[2]

Despite the use of English as the base language of the Internet, expansion of the World Wide Web outside the West has been substantial. An estimated 60% of the world's online population resides outside the United States. In Asia alone, the number of Internet users has grown to 64 million in 2003, and is expected to reach 370 million by 2006.[3] By 2005, non-English-speaking countries will have more people online than English-speaking countries, and their percentage of total use will increase to 57% by 2005. [4]

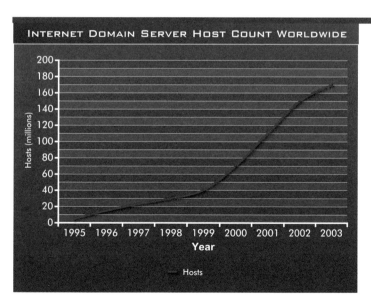

In the near future, the telecom industry will spearhead widespread use of wireless connectivity through handheld devices. Most mobile phones will provide Internet access, and the penetration of mobile devices with data capabilities will approach mobile phone user levels, especially in the United States, Western Europe, and Japan. The expansion will boost communication to new levels around the globe.

For businesses, global IT strategies have resulted in an accompanying economic transformation. Corporations have invested heavily in IT to reduce inefficiencies, accelerate product delivery, and enhance services through automated processes. Information sharing across business units has improved interaction and communication, making it easier for corporations to reposition in existing markets and enter into new markets.

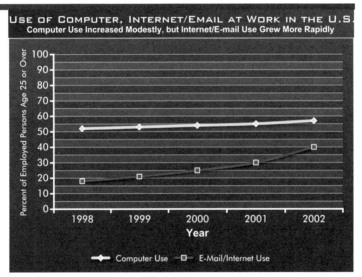

IT equipment purchase continues as the largest contributor to industry spending for all types of capital equipment costs. According to the NSF, industry expenditures on IT hardware and software rose from less than $200 billion in 1993 to more than $600 billion in 2000.[5] While this has slowed recently, it is expected to grow again.

IT requires a degree of education not previously needed for blue-collar, manufacturing positions. As it continues to grow, it will affect the unemployment and wage rates of skilled and unskilled labor. Education-based wage differentials have increased in the past two decades, coinciding with increased workplace computerization. Those differentials will likely become all the more pronounced in the years ahead. Businesses

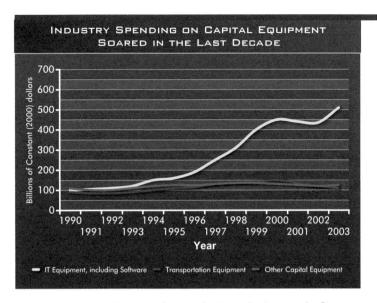

INDUSTRY SPENDING ON CAPITAL EQUIPMENT SOARED IN THE LAST DECADE

Billions of Constant (2000) dollars

— IT Equipment, including Software — Transportation Equipment — Other Capital Equipment

have had to invest in training and retraining their work forces — a trend that recurs every time a major IT innovation is widely adopted. Increasing wages and the relative supply of educated workers supports the belief that IT also improves productivity for skilled workers.

Governments also employ management information systems and IT research. In the industrialized world, IT has become a primary means of communication among governments, citizens, and public service providers. Transparency has increased as government information and civil society responses to public programs become increasingly available online. According to the NSF, the U.S. Treasury Department now collects two-thirds or $1.3 trillion of its Federal revenue electronically. By 1999, the Federal Government was making 96% of salary payments, 81% of vendor payments, and 73% of benefit payments electronically.[6] This movement from paper to electronic-based processing of documents and payments has generated cost savings of at least 50%. These gains are not limited to the United States, as advanced countries such as Japan and many Western European nations have also scheduled most government administrative services to go online. [7]

As public services adopt IT, they must protect individual privacy and ensure national security. For example, as more countries implement electronic voting, they will need to meet a host of security, privacy, and equity requirements. Internet hacking is now a federal offense in the United States, and it is likely that over time federal regulations and laws will develop to meet new demands imposed by advancements in, and the adoption of, new information technologies.

IT also impacts education. IT credentialing has risen, as evidenced by the 1.6 million people who earned nearly 2.4 million IT certifications in the last 15 years.[8] Furthermore, an increasing number of universities and colleges around the world are implementing distance education initiatives. The Massachusetts Institute of Technology (MIT) was the first major university to offer all of its core courses online, free to any student anywhere in the world with an Internet connection. Distance education creates new markets for companies and universities. These advancements make education available to anyone with Internet access, and provide students with a global network of information to supplement their knowledge and research.

Now and into the future, education, communication, information flows, and business transactions will benefit from advancements in information technology. Given the rapid rate of IT uptake by nearly every industry in the world, no company can afford to ignore the trends unfolding in this technological arena. Businesses worldwide should make the development and adoption of information technology a top priority.

BIOTECHNOLOGY

CHAPTER
nine

Throughout the 1990s, the introduction of genetically modified (GM) corn to U.S. markets, the human genome project, and the births of cloned animals sparked worldwide debate about biotechnology — the science used to alter the genetic constitution of plants and animals to improve their health, quality, and utility. While some countries consider biotechnology to represent the next revolution in medicine and agriculture, others have labeled genetically modified organisms (GMOs) as "genetic pollution" and have banned GM products. Skeptics have pointed out that little is known about the long-term effects of genetic modification on health and environment, while scientists continue to develop countless ideas of possible new biotechnology applications. This technology has the potential to impact a wide range of industries over the next 30 years.

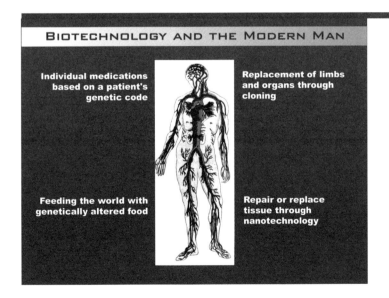

Since its commercial advent, the uptake of GM crops has been astounding. Commercial growers who have adopted the technology favor a diversity of GM crops, many of which have been made impervious to pests, herbicides, and even drought. As of 2002, 75% of soybeans, 33% of corn, and 70% of cotton grown in the United States were genetically modified cultivars.[1] Eighty percent of Canadian farmers have tested GM canola, and of this number, only 10–15% reverted to traditional varieties.[2] Given the success of bioengineered crops, growers and consumers have come to expect an abundance of high-quality farm products from GM harvests.

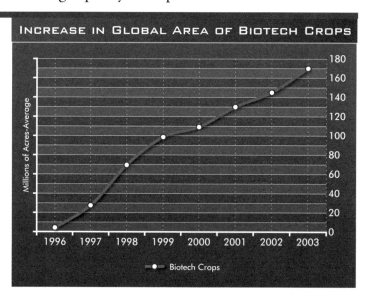

Though GM cultivars were the first biotech products to enter food supplies and markets, a host of other animal products and applications await approval and release. Salmon have been genetically engineered to develop faster, grow larger, and reproduce more frequently. Genetically altered trees support the demands of the paper industry by reaching maturity faster, and with improved pulp consistency.

Plants modified to absorb arsenic and purify polluted soils have been tested in India. Golden rice expresses vitamin A, a critical nutrient missing in the diets of many rural Asians.[3] The Food and Agriculture Organization (FAO) notes that advances in such "biofortification" and GM products could boost food production while increasing dietary diversification worldwide.[4]

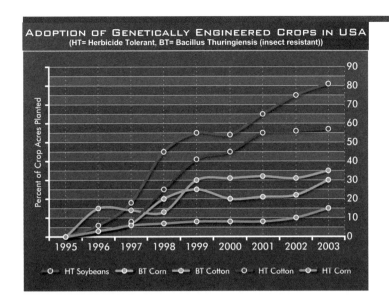

ADOPTION OF GENETICALLY ENGINEERED CROPS IN USA
(HT= Herbicide Tolerant, BT= Bacillus Thuringiensis (insect resistant))

○ HT Soybeans ● BT Corn ● BT Cotton ○ HT Cotton ● HT Corn

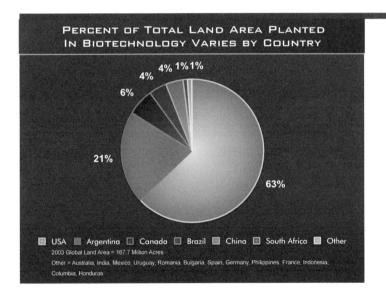

PERCENT OF TOTAL LAND AREA PLANTED
IN BIOTECHNOLOGY VARIES BY COUNTRY

■ USA ■ Argentina ■ Canada ■ Brazil ■ China ■ South Africa ■ Other

2003 Global Land Area = 167.7 Million Acres

Other = Australia, India, Mexico, Uruguay, Romania, Bulgaria, Spain, Germany, Philippines, France, Indonesia, Columbia, Honduras

Scientists also use biotechnology in the development of new medical procedures. Since the inception of the Human Genome Project in 1990, nearly all of the 30,000 human genes have been identified. This research has yielded a new approach to medicine termed "gene therapy." With the genes and trigger genes for certain diseases identified, doctors could screen patients' DNA to determine their susceptibility to disease. Genetic mutations could then be replaced or repaired with engineered and healthy genes. Some assert that babies in the womb could eventually be cured of genetic disorders before they are born.[5] Such suggestions have unsurprisingly resulted in a torrent of moral arguments over privacy, health insurance, and religion. Many are concerned that researchers will develop the technology to engineer traits such as intelligence or athleticism. Without a doubt, the rate of scientific advancement over the last 15 years has outpaced existing legal and regulatory systems.

Biotech research and development may also yield less expensive and more abundant supplies of medication. Experiments in which common animals, such as pigs, are used to produce medicine, show promise. It is hoped that drugs expressed in transgenic animal milk, blood, or tissues could be harvested for human use. Human-like hemoglobin, for instance, can now be made from swine blood and used as substitutes for transfusions. It is estimated that drugs developed in animals will be two to three times less expensive than medicines produced from cell cultures, the current method of production.[6] Though far off, scientists also hope to grow organs for human transplants in animals, thereby lowering the cost and increasing the availability of organs.

Given the implications of these advances, civil society groups have entered into heated debate about the safety and morality of biotechnology. At present, little is known about how GM plants and animals will impact biodiversity, ecosystem stability, and health in the long term. In agriculture, the EU maintains a ban on GM cultivars, contending that the products have not been proven safe for human consumption. Because of concern over GMOs, Zimbabwe and Zaire refused to import genetically modified food aid from the West to help relieve a recent food crisis.[7]

The advent of cloning, gene therapy, and engineered medications has further divided supporters and opponents of biotechnology. Although the emerging technologies show incredible promise for advancing modern medicine, society has not yet come to terms with the health, legal, moral, and religious ramifications of these new applications.

Many realize that regulatory systems must be upgraded before government institutions can effectively manage this nascent technology. The need for new laws and enforcement mechanisms was recently corroborated when Adventis Corporation accidentally allowed Starlink, a variety of GM corn not approved for human consumption, to enter the food supply. The incident cost the company millions of dollars and alerted many to the difficulty of containing and controlling biotech products.[8] It is not surprising that the public remains wary of pharmaceutical companies that are interested in engineering crops and farm animals to produce drugs.

It is well recognized that biotechnology research and development holds considerable promise for corporations and governments worldwide. The technology, implemented properly and with appropriate risk management, could mitigate a number of global problems, such as disease and hunger. Corporations that develop safe biotech applications will reap enormous profits if their products gain acceptance from a wary public. Public trust in GMOs will come only from enhanced measures to control misuse, sound risk-analysis programs, and advances in corporate transparency. The pace of development in the biotechnology industry will be largely governed by civil society's acceptance of GM products.

NANOTECHNOLOGY

CHAPTER
ten

The next force that we expect to have a global tectonic effect is, ironically, so small that it cannot be seen with the human eye. Nanotechnology is used to rearrange molecules so that essentially every atom can be put in its most efficient place. Dr. Ralph Merkle of the Georgia Institute of Technology describes it this way: "Manufactured products are made from atoms and the properties of those products depend on how those atoms are arranged. If we rearrange the atoms in coal, we can make diamond. If we rearrange the atoms in sand and add a few other trace elements, we can make computer chips. If we rearrange the atoms in dirt, water, and air, we can make potatoes."[1]

We are only now beginning to see the wide uses for this nascent technology. A recent book by Jack Uldrich and Deb Newberry put it this way:

> "This is not to say that nanotechnology is a far-off, fuzzy, futuristic technology. It is not. It has already established a beachhead in the economy. The clothing industry is starting to feel the effects of nanotech. Eddie Bauer, for example, is currently using embedded nanoparticles to create stain-repellent khakis. This seemingly simple innovation will impact not only khaki-wearers, but dry cleaners, who will find their business declining; detergent makers, who will find less of their product moving off the shelf; and stain-removal makers, who will experience a sharp decrease in customers. This modest, fairly low-tech application of nanotechnology is just the small tip of a vast iceberg — an iceberg that threatens to sink even the 'unsinkable' companies."[2]

In the longer term, nanotechnologies could change the face of materials science by enabling scientists to develop stronger and lighter materials. They could open up ever more significant opportunities with respect to sensors and the widescale collection of information. Nanotech could eventually change the nature of health care — moving us from what GE has called a "see and treat" world to a "predict and prevent" world. Hundreds of other applications are under consideration.[3]

This emerging technology has already attracted considerable investment; more than 30 countries have launched public nanotechnology research and development (R&D) programs.[4] The OECD reports that government R&D funding grew fivefold between 1997 and 2002, to an estimated $2 billion per year.[5]

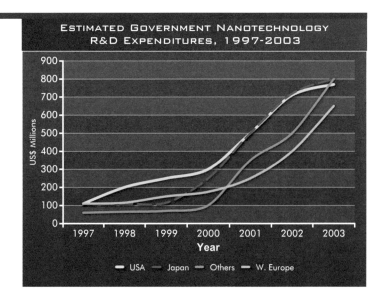

ESTIMATED GOVERNMENT NANOTECHNOLOGY
R&D EXPENDITURES, 1997-2003

In the private sector, large multinational firms, such as IBM, Dow Chemicals, L'Oreal, Hitachi, Unilever, and numerous start-up firms, have increased their nanotechnology research initiatives.

Patenting activity has also risen, with European Patent Office applications related to nanotechnology tripling between 1990 and1998, from 100 to 300 patents per annum.[6] The OECD believes this trend in patenting reflects the potentially large economic benefits from nanotechnology research.

Though patent applications and research initiatives have expanded quickly, the application of specific nanotechnologies has been limited. The tools and equipment to manufacture nanotech products require a precision found only in very costly machinery. As reported in MIT's

Technology Review, scientists are making headway, especially in the IT field, where nanotechnology creates considerable interest among computer chip manufacturers. Nanolithography, a high-tech printing process, can literally imprint nano (very small) patterns into silicon for future generations of high-speed processing. With this technology, computer scientists can now position more transistors onto a silicon wafer than current high-end lithography equipment.[7]

When perfected, advanced nanotechnology, also known as "molecular manufacturing," is expected to streamline production and reduce manufacturing costs so that they do not greatly exceed the cost of the required raw materials and energy. With every molecule in order, production will generate less waste and be more efficient, producing low-cost, high-quality nano-engineered products. These products, cheaper to buy and produce, have the potential to raise living standards around the world.[8] Mihail Roco, the National Science Foundation senior advisor on nanotechnology, predicts a future $1 trillion sales market for such nanotech components in the next 15 years.[9]

The medical sector is also working to develop and adopt "nanomedicines" that monitor, repair, construct, and control human biological systems at the molecular level. Treating the human body at the cellular level could allow doctors to develop new methods that could detect a number of cellular disorders, including many types of cancer.[9] Futuristic perhaps, nantotechology also increases the medical community's understanding of brain function. A nanostructured data storage device the size of a typical human liver cell could store information equivalent to the entire Library of Congress. Implanted in the human brain and equipped with appropriate interface mechanisms, this device could provide insights into brain function and artificial intelligence (AI) — the technology used to create intelligent robotic machines.[11]

Nanotechnological developments could also lead to a cleaner environment. The ability to create filtration systems at a molecularly precise level would improve purification of wastewater and gas from fossil fuels. Nanoparticles released into the atmosphere could help determine levels of atmospheric pollution and may even be helpful in detecting the presence of chemical and biological weapons.[12] Scientists also hope that advances in molecular manufacturing will develop solar power into a cost-effective energy solution.[13]

Consumer companies also understand the benefits of nanotechnology. Michael Mauboussin, a Credit Suisse First Boston analyst, conducted a survey of 30 Dow Jones companies to determine if companies were investigating or using nanotechnology. Based on his findings, Mauboussin predicts a rapidly growing corporate presence in the next decade. For example, while nanotech might not alter Coca-Cola's classic formula, nanotech-based advances in packaging materials for cans may provide better insulation to maintain cold temperatures and carbonation levels, resulting in increased product shelf life.

Nanotech may also affect retailers such as Home Depot and Wal-Mart. Nanotube-enhanced displays eliminate the need to change display signs manually. Instead, simple computer programming will adjust all store displays automatically. Nanotech-driven chip advances may eventually track food freshness and preparation time efficiency at McDonald's. Basing its operations on surface heat, surrounding heat, and food weight on the griddle, the technology may be able to determine the appropriate cooking time. While many of these examples now sound farfetched, companies have already employed nanotechnology to tailor the design and function of consumer products such as sunscreen and cosmetics.[14]

As with all new technologies, nanotechnology must be developed and implemented with proper risk assessment and regulation. Accidents caused by careless research and development can be avoided through the implementation of appropriate safety guidelines, in both the public and private sectors. Public education and business and government-sponsored discourse remain critical to the successful emergence of new nanotech applications. Such dialogue will result in improved regulation and safety enforcement, and wider public support for new products and processes utilizing the technology. Given the potential for nanotechnology to improve the manufacture, sale, and transport of goods and services, business leaders should spearhead efforts to mainstream and employ this technology as it develops.

SECTION FOUR

Conflict
and
Government

CHAPTER
eleven

Conflict is one of the Global Tectonic forces transforming the fundamentals of international business. During the last 40 years, with the end of the Cold War, the toppling of the Berlin Wall, and Soviet Russia's disintegration, international conflict has morphed from a bilateral clash between world superpowers into multiple civil and intrastate conflicts, many of which are clustered in the least developed countries of the world. The world has also seen the rise of terrorism and cyberterrorist strikes that threaten the world's vast computer networks.

Civil and intrastate conflicts and terrorist attacks have resulted in massive direct economic costs with significant threats to regional and international political and economic stability. The debilitating effects of conflict on economic development include massive, cross-border refugee

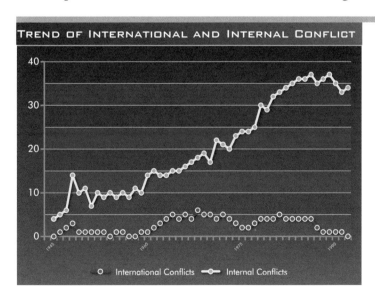

flows, increasing levels of disease in refugee camps and the disruption of food and medical aid to those most in need. Considerable transnational and civil strife occurs in politically and economically marginal countries, causing these countries to record little to no economic growth as military spending balloons and political instability dampens foreign investment and tourism.

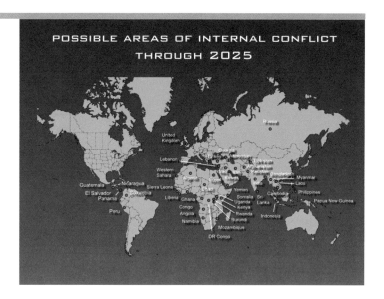

Countries that cannot provide basic services and resources to their populace are prone to civil unrest. Similarly, countries mired in conflict cannot attract foreign capital, dedicate their budgets to military spending, and are susceptible to long-term poverty. These countries will only be able to restore civil society and reinvigorate their ailing economies if they can establish stable governments and peace.

Since the fall of the Berlin Wall in 1989, more than 4 million people have been killed in internal and regional forms of conflict.[1] But only recently has the internal conflict of poor countries become a focal point for political discourse. Throughout the past 15 years, these countries experiencing violent conflict through rising ethnic, religious, and border strife have also become breeding grounds for terrorism.

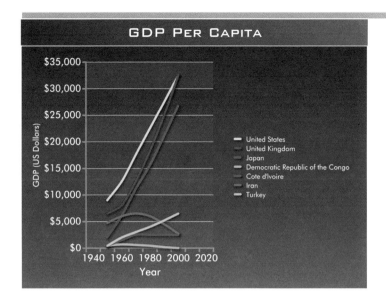

GDP PER CAPITA

The lack of economic opportunities, coupled with a bleak outlook for the future, both economically for the state and for the individual, tends to fuel the development of internal conflicts.

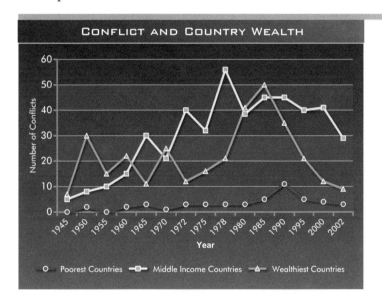

CONFLICT AND COUNTRY WEALTH

Developed countries like Japan, the United States, and members of the European Union have high and rising Gross Domestic Products (GDPs) per capita. In the last 40 years, the GDP of the United States has risen 3.5 times, while the United Kingdom's GDP is up sixfold and Japan's is up an astounding twentyfold. The same increasing standard of living cannot be said of the majority of Africa and the Middle East. In fact, it is just the opposite. During the same time period, the GDP of the Congo, Cote d'Ivoire, Saudi Arabia, Iran, and Kuwait have all gone down, with those countries experiencing a decline in their people's standard of living.[2]

The developed countries of the West provide economic opportunity that simply does not exist in the vast majority of Africa and the Middle East. Such low-income, low-growth countries are incubators for terrorist activities. Internal conflict and extremist groups tend to develop in this area of the world. Additional economic opportunities need to be developed in these marginal countries of the world in order to reduce conflict.

Conflict can also be reduced by giving people a voice in their own governance. Countries that are democratic have lower incidences of poverty, economic disparity, and thus conflict and terrorist development. In the past 50 years, the number of democratic governments in the world has increased fivefold. When a democratic government is in place, terrorist and nuclear arms development decrease. For instance, South Africa, a new democracy, recently dismantled its nuclear program, citing the prohibitive costs involved.

This dismantling of one of the eight nuclear arms programs in the world is good news. The very fact that just eight nuclear arms programs in the world exists is good news. The world has done a good job to date containing nuclear proliferation. Through the efforts of the United Nations' International Atomic Energy Agency (IAEA), the number of countries that have acquired the ability to make nuclear weapons has been held to eight — or possibly nine, if North Korea has indeed obtained the necessary ability, as has been recently reported in media throughout the world. Nine countries with nuclear capabilities is far fewer than what was imagined in the 1960s. In the early 1960s, President John F. Kennedy said that by 1975, there might be 20 nuclear powers. Today, 40 years later, there may be just nine.[3]

In addition to nuclear threats from governments, a high threat exists for a nuclear strike by one of the world's terrorist groups. Dangerous nuclear materials and facilities must be tightly controlled and secured from both rogue nations and terrorist groups.

Many heads of state have made it a priority to prevent terrorists from

○ PURSUING OR CAN ACQUIRE WEAPONS   ● POSSESSION OR POSSIBLE POSSESSION

STATE	NUCLEAR	CHEMICAL	BIOLOGICAL	MISSILE
ALGERIA	○			
BELARUS	○			
BULGARIA			●	
CHILE		●		
CHINA	●	●	●	●
CUBA			○	
ETHIOPIA		●		
EGYPT		●	●	●
FRANCE	●	●		
INDIA	●	●	○	●
INDONESIA		●		
IRAN	○	●	●	●
ISRAEL	●	●	●	●
KAZAKHSTAN	○			
LAOS		●	●	
LIBYA		●	●	●
MYANMAR		●		
NORTH KOREA	●	●	●	●
PAKISTAN	●	●	○	●
ROMANIA			○	
RUSSIA	●	●	●	●
SERBIA	○	●		
SOUTH AFRICA	○	●	●	●
SOUTH KOREA		●	●	●
SUDAN		●		
SYRIA		●	●	●
TAIWAN		●	○	●
THAILAND		●		
UKRAINE	○			
VIETNAM		●	●	
UNITED KINGDOM	●	●		●
UNITED STATES	●	●	●	●

gaining access to nuclear and biological weapons of mass destruction. Policymakers around the world now dedicate substantial resources to the war on terrorism. Governments are taking — and must continue to take — steps to strengthen their own domestic security.

World business leaders also cannot overlook governmental warnings on terrorism, especially given the costs of violence. The September 11 terrorist attacks on the United States resulted in an estimated $105 billion in immediate damages, including loss of life, destruction of property, and short-term depression of economic activity.[4] The prolonged threat of terrorism compounds these losses. Under continued threats of violence, consumer confidence decreases, perceived investor risk and interest rates increase, fuel prices become unpredictable, and critical industries such as airlines, restaurants, and tourist services falter. Given the ever-increasing economic integration of countries, attacks in one nation often reverber-

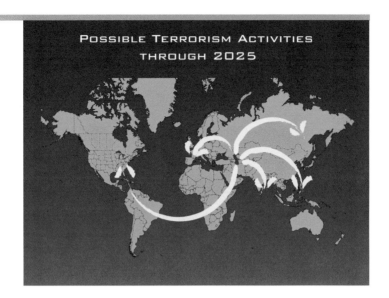

POSSIBLE TERRORISM ACTIVITIES THROUGH 2025

ate throughout the international business system, causing regional economic depression. According to an Asia-Pacific Economic Cooperation paper, "A study of 200 countries from 1968 to 1979 showed that a doubling in the number of terrorist incidents decreased bilateral trade between targeted economies by approximately 6 percent." In 2002, after the Bali tragedy, Indonesia lost approximately 1 percent of its GDP receipts. These examples illustrate the severe impact of terrorism on international business.[6]

The business implications of terrorism go beyond physical forms of conflict and terrorism and now extend to rising threats from cyberterrorism. Special consideration must now be given to safeguarding the information systems and computer networks—run by governments and businesses—that oversee almost every mechanism of modern society. Though not nearly as devastating as violent conflict, cyberterrorism poses a substantial threat to every computer-dependent firm in the world. During the past several years, the American government has taken a more proactive effort in fighting cyberterrorism. In 1999, the United States committed $1.46 billion to fight cyberterrorism.[7] Today, nearly every important corporation is computer dependent, making cyberterrorism a real threat to world business. By hitting the twin towers of New York's World Trade Center, terrorists sought to cripple America's economic prosperity, and by disrupting the U.S. computer systems, they could conceivably achieve that goal.

Given the rise of civil conflict, the escalation of terrorism, and the frequency of Internet hacking, companies need to develop increased security standards and policies around the world. Such precautions will raise the costs of shipping, production, and internal protection on a global scale. In light of new security requisites, corporations will need to collaborate with governments to devise clear and substantive measures to prevent terrorists from gaining access to new technologies, and to protect their operations. The business world must recognize terrorism as a growing challenge to the entire global system.

While in recent years, conflict, terrorism, and cyberterrorism have become widely debated topics of high concern, many believe steps toward peace are made every day. Although we will never totally rid the world of conflict, we can make significant progress toward that objective if people are allowed to have a voice in their own future through democratic governments. With more than 60 percent of the world's nations now governed by democracies, there is hope that the future may bring a reduction in conflicts of all types. Success in democratization of the poorer countries in Africa and the Middle East will go far in reducing conflict and terror.

GOVERNANCE

CHAPTER
twelve

For the majority of history, enhanced governance meant improving the leadership of nation-states. Classic reforms changed how governments instituted law, taxation, and social welfare. In the early 1900s, however, the rise of multinational corporations (MNCs) changed the system of governance and the struggle for social and economic reform and progress. Corporations such as United Fruit, Inc., which benefited from the global advance of democracy and capitalism, grew into large and powerful enterprises.[1] In just a few decades, multinational companies rivaled some governments as influential actors in state policy and decision making.

By the mid- to late-1900s, MNCs themselves had become agents of governance and targets for reform.[2] Their policies had enormous impact on the economic well-being of the states in which they operated — as well as the livelihoods of their vast pools of employees in countries across the world. Progressively, corporations have been regarded as more than wealth-maximization entities. Instead, as they have expanded their profile in countries and regions across the world, MNCs have been the target of various labor and other groups for efforts to effect broader social, economic, and political change.[3] Today, civil society continues to press for reforms in corporate patterns — from corporate citizenship to corporate social responsibility to what Procter & Gamble refers to as "corporate social opportunity." [4]

Toward the end of the twentieth century, a third actor — the nongovernmental organization (NGO) — rapidly began to influence corporate and state governance. As an outgrowth of democracy, the NGO has grown as a mechanism by which civil society can seek to increase its control over corporate and government decision making. Groups such as Consumers Union, CorpWatch, Greenpeace International, Policy Action Network, and Public Citizen have captured the support of youth and many consumer and other groups. They have leveraged the revolution in information technology to force transparency on traditionally closed companies and governments. Their popular support and charge of information has made NGOs a current and powerful addition to world governance system. Over the next 25 years, we expect NGOs, multinationals, and governments to be both catalysts for and targets of governance reform. The interaction of these actors will give rise to three major governance trends: the spread of democracy, improved corporate governance, and the con-

tinued emergence of NGOs as corporate and government watchdogs. These changes in governance will impact internal business processes and shape the international environment in which corporations trade and invest. To remain viable in the future, business leaders will need to adjust their corporate strategies to address these inevitable political, corporate, and civil developments.

Democracy and broader political participation will continue to spread in the world, improving conditions for market-based economies. Multinational companies realize benefits from democratization, especially as governments committed to sound political and economic policies create more open, fair, and efficient business environments. In 1950, only 22 of 154 countries (14.3%) were identified as democracies, but by 2000 the count had increased to 119 of 192 (62%).[5] Moreover, these states have expressed their commitment to democracy through a number of international mechanisms. The by-product is the consolidation of democratic principles and procedures and a reinforcing network by which democratic practices generally are rewarded by higher civil freedoms on the one hand, and more efficient economic systems and standards of living on the other.

For instance, between 1990 and 2001, the percentage of states that ratified the six major human rights conventions and covenants grew from 10% to 50% of all countries. As of January 1, 2002, 144 nations had gained membership in the World Trade Organization (WTO).[6] Though the transition to democracy can be a long and harried process, many countries are becoming freer societies with improved rule of law and economic transparency. This trend is expected to continue throughout the next 25 years and beyond. The inevitable conclusion is that liberal democracy and capitalism have prevailed. They have been reaffirmed at a time when communism, authoritarianism, and statism and central-control economic systems have been abandoned by a large part of the world. This nearly systematic renunciation of other models suggests that the scholar Francis Fukuyama got it right when he argued at the time of the collapse of the Soviet Union that we had reached the "end of history" insofar as we had seen the collapse of all other significant alternatives to liberal democracy and capitalism. [7]

With more countries adopting internationally accepted rules and policies, multinational companies (MNCs) will benefit from larger and improved operating environments at home and abroad. For all business stakeholders, capital, labor, commodities, technology, and information will flow more freely across borders. In addition, MNCs will actively promote further democratic reform in their client countries. For example, in the most recent round of WTO negotiations, MNCs pushed their host governments to negotiate international agreements on investment and intellectual property rights.[8] Such standards and regulations, if fairly implemented, will improve corporate profitability as well as boost foreign direct investment in a wide range of host countries.

In spite of these expected advancements in the area of governance, many countries around the world will maintain rule-based systems and institutions that hinder business development. In a number of developing countries, excessive business regulation and complex procedural systems will result in the slowdown of business. In Egypt, for example, a person who wants to legally register his ownership of state-owned desert land must overcome 77 bureaucratic procedures at 31 public and private agencies in a process that takes 5–14 years. In Haiti, becoming a rightful owner of land can take 19 years. [9]

Many legal systems in developing countries have become unwieldy, causing businesses to grow and operate extra-legally. Since 1990, 85% of all new jobs in Latin America and the Caribbean were created in the extra-legal sector— i.e., people working for, or running, businesses that have not met government requirements for registration, land ownership, or operation. In Zambia, for example, only 10% of the workforce is legally employed. [10]

When legal and social systems create barriers to entrepreneurship, both local and international companies become vulnerable to expropriation, bribery, and crime. Replacing legal uncertainty with sound jurisprudence, property rights, and good governance will greatly enhance local and international investment in developing countries around the world. Corporations will be more apt to initiate investments and build factories in countries where their rights are protected and where they do not lose profits and opportunities in a maze of legal obstacles.

Much like countries, MNCs will also pursue improvements in governance. The recent and quick expansion of the global market has given enormous power to these firms. In 2000, 51 of the top 100 economies of the world were corporations rather than nation-states, highlighting the need for adequate checks and balances on business operations.[11] In the wake of the Enron and WorldCom scandals, world leaders have realized that accountability and transparency in corporate governance cannot be overemphasized. Given the wealth and visibility of many MNCs, civil society, NGOs, and governments will likely intensify their efforts to pressure these business giants to exercise greater accountability and transparency in the next 25 years and beyond. This trend in corporate governance and in broader corporate "citizenship" — the ways in which MNCs engage in nonbusiness activities in communities — will create a new set of business values. Progressively, business leaders will not just make money for their stockholders. Instead, they will work for the interests of all of their stakeholders—employees, customers, suppliers, and the communities and countries in which they operate.

During the last two decades, NGOs have played an increasingly important role in the international business environment as corporate and government watchdogs. In the next two decades, these groups will become better organized, more media savvy, more active as stakeholders, and more connected to their constituencies by Internet and telecommunication technologies.

The effects of these changes are already visible, dramatic, and widespread. For instance, Nike Corporation, under pressure for hiring cheap labor in substandard conditions, revamped its policy to be more in line with declarations on international labor standards and human rights.[12] ExxonMobil is paying billions to address the environmental and social damages caused after the Exxon-Valdez oil tanker crashed and spilled crude oil off the coast of Alaska.[13] Through public education and information dissemination, NGOs can pressure governments and corporations to be more accountable and transparent about issues ranging from human rights to environment to labor standards. Corporations cannot afford to ignore these organizations that have the backing of a younger generation of civil society and the power to report information quickly and accurately. Nongovernmental organizations have garnered a great deal of influence in global society, and they will continue to shape corporate governance.

As they grow in power, NGOs will also be required to meet international and local accountability and transparency standards. These organizations will need to maintain a balance between volunteerism and activism (a defining characteristic of NGOs) and to develop and maintain the professionalism necessary to operate competitively in nonprofit and business environments. The United Nations, for instance, has adopted a program of NGO certification, thereby elevating the credibility of its nongovernmental partners. In the future, NGOs that desire to maintain their social influence will have to meet high reporting standards in addition to providing further public access to their funding sources and affiliations.

Looking forward, we also expect NGOs themselves to experience a period of pronounced pressure on their own governance structures not dissimilar to what the private sector experienced in the wake of the Enron events. Looming issues such as legitimacy (where do NGOs get their authority?) and operational characteristics (how efficiently are they operated?) will assume ever-sharper definition.

Now and into the future, NGOs, multinational companies, and governments will become more accountable and transparent. During the next few decades, advancements in governance will unfold like the domino effect: Businesses will challenge governments to improve the rule of law; governments will more tightly regulate corporate operations; and NGOs will report to civil society on both business and country proceedings. As they unfold, these trends in governance will improve the quality, dignity, and efficiency of international business across the globe.

CONCLUSION

Global
Tectonics

Global Trends: Conclusion

Many of these Global Tectonics, by virtue of their gradual nature, will fail to capture headlines. Many of these forces, because they will be long-range in nature, will never be the subject of debate in boardrooms dominated by shorter-term concerns. Many, because they will have subtle and gradual effects, will be overshadowed by other day-to-day events. And many, because they will unfold slowly, will go unnoticed by governments, companies, and other organizations.

The reality, however, is that each of the Global Tectonic forces that we have described here can be expected to have a significant impact on how the world unfolds in the years ahead. Each can be expected to play a significant role in determining how we live, the nature and rate of economic activity around us, the ways in which we interact with other people, and, ultimately, the prospects that we provide for our children and grandchildren. Each carries with it simultaneous dangers and opportunities. And each tectonic will have a number of inflection points — points at which leadership decisions will mean the difference between success and failure.

Especially in light of these longer-range trends, businesses need to be "tuned in" to these geopolitical tectonic trends if they are to stay competitive. More and more, we believe, the capacity to anticipate and adapt business operations to these trends will be an increasingly critical comparative advantage. In short, the outlook for businesses will increasingly be contingent on their capacity to develop and implement a strategic vision in the face of ever more onerous shorter-term pressures. That is no small task.

The record suggests that this kind of innovation in long-range positioning carries with it high premiums. We believe that the premiums associated with rapid innovation will be even more significant in the future — as the forces of creative destruction continue to reward rapid adapters and as the same forces simply remove slow or nonadapters from the picture.

There are many compelling examples of companies that have succeeded or failed as a result of their capacity to adapt to changing conditions. There will be many more. Recently, the rapid development and diffusion of technology is the obvious force that has fundamentally transformed the marketplace. Other forces, as we have argued, will follow. The winners and losers will be determined by their capacity to innovate: first, to innovate in the framework of their operations to exploit the changing business environment, and second and more importantly, to adapt their strategies to account for anticipated change.

These dynamics, we expect, will apply not only to companies but also to governments — both big and small — and other organizations, ranging from NGOs to educational institutions. The outlook for these groups will also be determined by the degree to which they can look forward — to the various trends at work and the ways in which they can recalibrate their goals and operations to reflect the world they expect to see.

Moreover, we wish to stress the complexities inherent in these broad global trends and emphasize the need to avoid generalizations and broad-brush conclusions. For example, by dividing the world along "developed" country and "developing" country lines, with all the methodological and other ambiguities that implies, there is the danger that the complexities associated with the global tectonics — the granularities within and between these groups — will be lost. To draw from our discussion of water as a strategic resource of the future, a compelling example of this point is China. Beijing has one of the largest stocks of freshwater in the world; it is among the world's most significant water "powers." But at the same time, the country is challenged by very significant stratifications — stratifications between its population size (some 20% of the world population) and water stocks (an estimated 8% of the world's freshwater), stratifications between urban and rural, and stratifications between water availability for economic use (agricultural versus industrial).

The bottom line is that organizations need more than just vision. They need good, effective vision that can differentiate between salient elements and the "background noise" of less important elements that serve to clutter their capacity to navigate. They need to appreciate the granularity of the many tectonic forces around them, but without losing the big picture. By definition, it is a significant challenge to develop and then maintain such effective vision, let alone ensure that it is implemented operationally.

In this kind of environment, when strategic vision carries with it a high premium and the need for effective strategic insight is all the more significant, it becomes all the more unexplainable that leaders seem to be focused on the short term. Fewer and fewer organizations engage in long-range planning, especially with a view to assessing the long-range forces unfolding across the planet. Planning horizons have become shorter, and the capacity of leaders to take the long view is constrained by a constellation of relentless short-term metrics they must face, ranging from political election cycles to quarterly profit statements. This amounts to increasingly myopic management at a time when farsighted leadership is necessary.

This epidemic of "short-termism" transcends the private sector. Leaders in the "dot-gov" and "dot-org" world are also subject to many of the same pressures that together serve to crowd out thinking about the many important gradual drivers of change. It is not inconceivable that we could see the equivalent of an Enron shake-out in the nonprofit sphere, for example, as leadership structures and modes of operation are subject to higher levels of scrutiny. At the level of nation-states, we see the trend of higher "hurdle rates" of governance — higher standards applied to the way government structures across the world carry out their constituent functions.

This short monograph, which frames some of the big tectonic forces at work and illuminates some of the future challenges we face, is intended to offer leaders some thinking about these longer-range forces. It is not exhaustive. Nor is it detailed. We have undertaken this monograph to highlight some of the global forces that need further examination, to examine and assign priorities to the range of drivers of change that we confront, and to sketch the outlines for more detailed work that both the Center for Global Business Studies at Penn State University and the Global Strategy Institute at the Center for Strategic and International Studies are committed to launching.

These Global Tectonics will continue to evolve, shift, and change the fundamental nature of business as we know it. With this effort to identify the major tectonic plates, we now need to dig deeper and detail the impacts of these trends on various industries. Case studies of different corporations can teach us how successful companies will adapt, and why other companies will be swallowed by tectonic fissures.

APPENDIX

Sources

1. Population Reference Bureau "Human Population: Fundamentals of Growth - Natural Increase and Future Growth."
http://www.prb.org/Content/NavigationMenu/PRB/Educators/Human_Population/Future_Growth/Natural_Increase_and_Future_Growth.htm#growth (September 2004).

2. U.S. Census Database "Total Midyear Population for the World: 1950–2050."
http://www.census.gov/ipc/www/worldpop.html (September 2004).

3. United Nations Population Fund (UNFPA) "Population Issues." www.unfpa.org (September 2004).

4. Chamie, Joseph "Statement to the Commission on Population and Development." United Nations. March 22, 2004.   https://www.un.org/esa/population/cpd/37OPEN.pdf (September 2004).

5. Lutz, Wolfgang "The End of World Population Growth in the 21st Century: New Challenges for Human Capital Formation and Sustainable Development." International Institute for Applied Systems Analysis. July 2004.   http://www.iiasa.ac.at/Research/POP/pub/worldbook04.html (September 2004).

6. United Nations Population Fund "Population and Demographic Dynamics." www.unfpa.org/index.htm (September 2004).

7. U.S. Census Bureau "World Population at a Glance 2002 and Beyond." March 2004.
www.census.gov/ipc/prod/wp02/wp02-1.pdf (Sep 2004).

8. U.S. Census Bureau "IDB Aggregation". http://www.census.gov/ipc/www/idbagg.html (September 2004).

9. National Intelligence Council "Global Trends 2015." December 2000.
http://www.cia.gov/cia/reports/globaltrends2015/ (September 2004).

10. Kinsella and Velkoff "An Aging World, 2001: International Population Reports." U.S. Bureau of the Census. Nov 2001. http://www.census.gov/prod/2001pubs/p95-01-1.pdf (September 2004).

11. Kinsella and Velkoff "An Aging World, 2001: International Population Reports." U.S. Bureau of the Census. Nov 2001. http://www.census.gov/prod/2001pubs/p95-01-1.pdf (September 2004).

12. Kinsella and Velkoff "An Aging World, 2001: International Population Reports." U.S. Bureau of the Census. Nov 2001. http://www.census.gov/prod/2001pubs/p95-01-1.pdf (September 2004).

GRAPHS

1.1: The Growth of World Population
U.S. Census Database "Total Midyear Population for the World: 1950–2050."
http://www.census.gov/ipc/www/worldpop.html (September 2004).

1.2: Growth Rate of World Population by Region, 2004–2025
U.S. Census Bureau, "International Data Base."
http://www.census.gov/cgi-bin/ipc/idbsprd (September 2004).
http://www.census.gov/ipc/www/idbagg.html (September 2004).

1.3: The Growth of World Population LDC vs. MDC, 1950–2025
Population Division of the Department of Economic and Social Affairs of the United Nations Secretariat "World Population Prospects: The 2002 Revision and World Urbanization Prospects: The 2001 Revision." http://esa.un.org/unpp, (September 2004).

1.4: Age Structure of World Population 2000 vs. 2025
See 1.3

1.5: Youth Bulge Status in 2025
See 1.2

1.6: Countries with Declining Population 2004 vs. 2025
See 1.2

1.7: Migration of World Population
Population Reference Bureau "Population Bulletin: Transitions in World Population." March 2004.
http://www.prb.org/Template.cfm?Section=PRB&template=/ContentManagement/ContentDisplay.cfm&ContentID=10610. (September 2004).

1.8: Dependency Ratios of More Developed Countries, 2004 vs. 2025
U.S. Census Bureau, "International Data Base."
http://www.census.gov/cgi-bin/ipc/idbsprd (September 2004).
http://www.census.gov/ipc/www/idbagg.html (September 2004).

CHAPTER TWO: URBANIZATION

1. The Population Institute "The Issue—Urbanization." http://www.populationinstitute.org/teampublish/71_234_1058.cfm (September 2004).

2. United Nations "World Urbanization Prospects: The 2003 Revision." 2003. http://www.un.org/esa/population/publications/wup2003/2003WUPHighlights.pdf (September 2004).

3. United Nations "World Urbanization Prospects: The 2003 Revision." 2003. http://www.un.org/esa/population/publications/wup2003/2003WUPHighlights.pdf (September 2004).

4. United Nations "World Urbanization Prospects: The 2003 Revision." 2003. http://www.un.org/esa/population/publications/wup2003/2003WUPHighlights.pdf (September 2004).

5. United Nations Educational, Scientific and Cultural Organization "Mega Cities of the World." Aug 17, 2001. http://www.unesco.org/culture/worldreport/html_eng/graph8.shtml (September 2004).

GRAPHS

2.1: Share of Regional Populations in Urban Areas 2000 vs. 2030
United Nations "World Urbanization Prospects: The 2003 Revision". 2003. http://www.un.org/esa/population/publications/wup2003/2003WUPHighlights.pdf (Sep 2004).

2.2: Urban Population by Region 2000 vs. 2030
See 2.1

2.3: Megacities of the World, 2015
United Nations Educational, Scientific and Cultural Organization "Megacities of the World." Aug. 17, 2001. http://www.unesco.org/culture/worldreport/html_eng/graph8.shtml (September 2004).

CHAPTER THREE: DISEASE AND GLOBALIZATION

1. The World Health Organization "Communicable Disease Surveillance and Response (CSR)." http://www.who.int/csr/don/2003_07_04/en/ (September 2004).

2. Roach, Stephan "Commentary on SARS April 7, 2003." Morgan Stanley. April 7, 2003.

3. Bartelme, Tony "Foreign Water a Growing Worry." The Post and Courier. Jan 19, 1997. http://archives.charleston.net/fish/fish7.html (September 2004).

4. CDC "CDC Telebriefing Transcript: Monkeypox Investigation." June 7, 2003. http://www.cdc.gov/od/oc/media/transcripts/t030607.htm (September 2004).

5. CSIS "World AIDS Summit Warns of Challenges Ahead." September 2002. http://www.globalization101.org/news.asp?NEWS_ID=35 (September 2004).

6. The World Bank Group "Public Health at a Glance: HIV/AIDS." http://wbln0018.worldbank.org/HDNet/hddocs.nsf/c840b59b6982d2498525670c004def60/0560436b70e56 de385256a4800524119?OpenDocument (September 2004).

7. UNAIDS, World Health Organization "AIDS Epidemic Update 2003." 2003. http://www.unaids.org/Unaids/EN/Resources/Publications/corporate+publications/aids+epidemic+update+-+december+2003.asp (September 2004).

8. National Intelligence Council "The Next Wave of HIV/AIDS: Nigeria, Ethiopia, Russia, India, and China." September 2002. http://www.fas.org/irp/nic/hiv-aids.html (September 2004).

9. Department of Homeland Security "Dark Winter Exercise." June 2001. http://www.homelandsecurity.org/darkwinter/index.cfm (September 2004).

GRAPHS

3.1 Estimated Population with HIV/AIDS 2003
UNAIDS, World Health Organization "AIDS Epidemic Update 2003." 2003. http://www.unaids.org/Unaids/EN/Resources/Publications/corporate+publications/aids+epidemic+update+-+december+2003.asp (Sept. 14, 2004).

3.2 Effect of HIV/AIDS on Life Expectancy 2010
Stanecki, Karen "The Aids Pandemic in the 21st Century". USAID. 2002. http://www.usaid.gov/our_work/global_health/aids/Publications/pandemic.pdf (Sept. 14, 2004).

CHAPTER FOUR: RESOURCE MANAGEMENT

1. The World Resources Institute "Key Publications Extracts." http://www.t21.ca/water/tp.htm (September 2004).

2. The World Resources Institute "Key Publications Extracts." http://www.t21.ca/water/tp.htm (September 2004).

3. International Energy Agency "World Energy Investment Outlook: Executive Summary." November 2003. http://www.worldenergyoutlook.org/weo/pubs/weio/English.pdf (September 2004).

Graphs

4.1 Water Stressed Countries 2000 to 2025
World Resource Institute "World Resources 2000–2001" http://www.wri.org (September 2004).

4.2 Incidence of Undernourishment in Developing Countries
The Food and Agriculture Organization of the United Nations "World Agriculture Towards 2015/2030, An FAO Perspective." 2000. http://www.fao.org/docrep/005/y4252e/y4252e00.htm (September 2004).

4.3 Number of Undernourished in the Developing World
See 4.2

4.4 World Total Energy Consumption, 1990–2020
The Energy Information Administration "International Energy Outlook 2004." April 2004
http://www.eia.doe.gov/pub/international/iealf/table18.xls, http://www.eia.doe.gov/oiaf/ieo/pdf/appa1_a8.pdf
(September 2004).

4.5 World Natural Gas Consumption by Region 2001 vs. 2025
The Energy Information Administration "Natural Gas." http://www.eia.doe.gov/oiaf/aeo/excel/aeotab_21.xls
(September 2004).

CHAPTER FIVE: ENVIRONMENTAL DEGRADATION

1. The United Nations Environment Program "Declaration on Environment and Development: Rio de Janeiro." June 3–14, 1992.
http://www.unep.org/Documents/Default.asp?DocumentID=78&ArticleID=1163 (September 2004).

2. The World Bank Group "The World Report 1992: Development and the Environment." September 1992.

3. The United Nations Convention on Climate Change. http://unfccc.int/text/resource (September 2004).

4. NationMaster.com. Statistics are user selected. www.nationmaster.com (September 2004).

5. The Environmental Protection Agency "Clear Skies Plan." http://www.epa.gov/clearskies/ (September 2004).

6. The United Nations Education, Cultural and Scientific Organization "The World Water Assessment Program." http://www.unesco.org/water/wwap/facts_figures/index.shtml (September 2004).

7. The United Nations Education, Cultural and Scientific Organization "The World Water Assessment Program." http://www.unesco.org/water/wwap/facts_figures/index.shtml (September 2004).

8. The United Nations Education, Cultural and Scientific Organization "The World Water Assessment Program." http://www.unesco.org/water/wwap/facts_figures/index.shtml (September 2004).

9. Ball, Jeffrey. "Honda, Toyota Plan to Release Fuel-Cell Test Vehicles in U.S." The Wall Street Journal. Dec 3, 2002. pg. D.8

10. "Showa Shell opens Tokyo's First Liquid Hydrogen Station" Shell Corporation Press Release. July 18, 2003. http://www.shell.com/home/Framework?siteId=pk-en&FC2=&FC3=/globalnews_and_library/pressreleases/2003/showa_shell_liquid_hydro_station_18062003.html (September 2004).

11. NASA "The Rate of Deforestation." The Earth Observatory.
http://earthobservatory.nasa.gov/Library/Deforestation/deforestation_2.html (September 2004).

12. Annan, Kofi "Message on the World Day to Combat Desertification." United Nations Convention to Combat Desertification. June 17, 2004. http://www.unccd.int/publicinfo/statement/annan2004.php (September 2004).

13. United Nations Convention to Combat Desertification. http://www.unccd.int/main.php (September 2004).

GRAPHS

5.1: World Carbon Dioxide Emissions
NationMaster.com (September 2004).

5.2: CO_2 Emissions by Region
Energy Information Administration, Office of Integrated Analysis and Forecasting "International Energy Outlook 2004." April 2004. www.eia.doe.gov/oiaf/ieo//index.html (September 2004).

5.3: Top Ten Countries with Highest Freshwater Pollution
See 5.1

5.4: Industrial Water Use Increases With Country Income
The United Nations Education, Cultural and Scientific Organization "The World Water Assessment Program." http://www.unesco.org/water/wwap/facts_figures/index.shrml (September 2004).

5.5: Evolution of Global Water Use
The United Nations Environment Programme "Water Use and Management." http://www.unep.org/vitalwater/management.htm (September 2004).

CHAPTER SIX: ECONOMIC INTEGRATION

1. Center for Strategic and International Studies "Seven Revolutions: Economic Integration." http://www.7revs.org/Econ/econ2.html (September 2004).

2. The Airbus Consortium Web site. http://www.airbus.com/ (September 2004).

3. Mak, Anthony. "Comparison of Revenues among Stats and TNCs." The Global Policy Organization. May 10, 2000. http://www.globalpolicy.org/socecon/tncs/tncstat2.htm (September 2004).

4. Holt, Benjamin "Main Recipients of Foreign Direct Investment." The Global Policy Organization. July 1999. http://www.globalpolicy.org/socecon/tncs/oiltable.htm (September 2004).

5. Anderson, Sarah and Cavanagh, John "Top 200 The Rise of Corporate Global Power." Institute for Policy Studies. Dec 2000. www.ips-dc.org/downloads/Top_100.pdf (September 2004).

6. Holt, Benjamin "Main Recipients of Foreign Direct Investment." The Global Policy Organization. July 1999. http://www.globalpolicy.org/socecon/tncs/oiltable.htm (September 2004).

7. "World Investment Report 2003: FDI Policies for Development: National and International Perspectives Chapter 3." The United Nations Conference on Trade and Development. 2003. http://www.unctad.org/en/docs/wir2003ch3_en.pdf (September 2004).

8. Dearaujo, Ernani "Chaotic Congo." Harvard International Review. Cambridge, Fall 2001. Vol 23; Iss 3 pg. 10.

9. "Jagdish Bhagwati Testimony: Subcommittee on Domestic and International Monetary Policy, Trade and Technology." April 1, 2003. http://financialservices.house.gov/media/pdf/040103jb.pdf (September 2004).

10. King. Neil. and Miller, Scott "Trade Talks Fail Amid Big Divide Over Farm Issues; Developing Countries Object to U.S., EU Goals; Cotton as a Rallying Cry." The Wall Street Journal. (Eastern edition). Sep 15, 2003. pg. A.1

11. Dearaujo, Ernani "Chaotic Congo." Harvard International Review. Cambridge, Fall 2001. Vol 23; Iss 3 pg. 10.

GRAPHS

6.1: Top 30 Economic Entities
Anderson, Sarah and Cavanagh, John "Top 30 Economic Entities." Top 200: The Rise of Corporate Global Power, Institute for Policy Studies. December 2000. www.ips-dc.org/downloads/Top_100.pdf (September 2004).

6.2: Geographical Distribution of FDI to EMCs 1990–2002
IMF "Foreign Direct Investment in Emerging Market Countries." Report of the Working Group of the Capital Markets Consultative Group. September 2003.
http://www.imf.org/external/np/cmcg/2003/eng/091803.pdf   (September 2004).

CHAPTER SEVEN: KNOWLEDGE DISSEMINATION

1. U.S. Department of Labor, Bureau of Labor Statistics "Fastest-Growing Industries." Feb. 11, 2004.
http://www.bls.gov/emp/empfastestind.htm (September 2004).

2. Breimyer, Frederick S. "The U.S. Manufacturing Sector: A Strong Past and an Uncertain Future." FDIC Outlook. Sept. 1, 2004. http://www.fdic.gov/bank/analytical/regional/ro20043q/na/2004fall_03.html (September 2004).

3. The World Bank Group "Poor Countries Pay Heavy Price for Growing Knowledge Gap." News Release, The World Bank Group. Dec. 4, 2002.
http://web.worldbank.org/WBSITE/EXTERNAL/NEWS/0,,contentMDK:20079404~menuPK:34465~page PK:64003015~piPK:64003012~theSitePK:4607,00.html (September 2004).

4. The World Bank Group "Poor Countries Pay Heavy Price for Growing Knowledge Gap." News Release, The World Bank Group. Dec. 4, 2002.
http://web.worldbank.org/WBSITE/EXTERNAL/NEWS/0,,contentMDK:20079404~menuPK:34465~page PK:64003015~piPK:64003012~theSitePK:4607,00.html (September 2004).

5. National Science Foundation "Science and Engineering Indicators 2002."
http://www.nsf.gov/sbe/srs/seind02/c2/c2s4.htm (September 2004).

6. International Recording Media Association "Statistics on Worldwide CD and DVD Replication."
http://www.recordingmedia.org/news/stat-replication_worldwide.html (September 2004).

7. IFPI "Commercial Piracy Report 2003." Representing the Recording Industry Worldwide.
http://www.ifpi.org/site-content/antipiracy/piracy2003-piacy-statistics.html (September 2004).

8. CNN "SoBig Worm Not Slowing Down Yet". Aug.21, 2003. http://money.cnn.com/2003/08/21/technology/sobig/index.htm?cnn=yes (September 2004).

GRAPHS

7.1: Relationship Between National Innovative Capacity and Prosperity
Stern, Porter and Furman "The Determinants of National Innovative Capacity." National Bureau of Economic Research. September 2000. www.nber.org/papers./w7876 (September 2004).

7.2: University Degrees in Science and Engineering Fields by Region
National Science Foundation "Science and Engineering Indicators 2002". 2002.
http://www.nsf.gov/sbe/srs/seind02/c2/c2s4.htm (September 2004).

7.3: U.S. vs. Asia Bachelor of Science and Engineering Degrees
See 7.2

7.4: International Patent Per Capita, Leading Countries
See 7.1

7.5: Correlation of Expected Duration of Schooling to National Wealth
United Nations Educational, Scientific and Cultural Organization "Global Education Digest." UNESCO Institute for Statistics. 2004. http://www.uis.unesco.org/TEMPLATE/pdf/ged/2004/GED2004_EN.pdf (September 2004).

CHAPTER EIGHT: INFORMATION TECHNOLOGY

1. The Center for Future Studies "Science and Technology Overview." 1999. http://www.futurestudies.co.uk/predictions/099.pdf (September 2004).

2. IDC "Percent of U.S. Households Owning Computers/Online." http://idc.com/ (September 2004).

3. IDC "Percent of U.S. Households Owning Computers/Online." http://idc.com/ (September 2004).

4. Opinionpower.com Surveys "Internet Statistics." 2004. http://www.opinionpower.com/statistics.html (September 2004).

5. NSF "Chapter 8: Significance of Information Technology." 2002. http://www.nsf.gov/sbe/srs/seind02/c8/c8s1.pdf (September 2004).

6. NSF "Chapter 8: Significance of Information Technology." 2002. http://www.nsf.gov/sbe/srs/seind02/c8/c8s1.pdf (September 2004).

7. NSF "Chapter 8: Significance of Information Technology." 2002. http://www.nsf.gov/sbe/srs/seind02/c8/c8s1.pdf (September 2004).

8. NSF "Chapter 8: Significance of Information Technology." 2002. http://www.nsf.gov/sbe/srs/seind02/c8/c8s1.pdf (September 2004).

Graphs

8.1: Moore's Law, 1971-2005
NSF "Chapter 8: Significance of Information Technology." 2002. http://www.nsf.gov/sbe/srs/seind02/c8/c8s1.pdf (September 2004).

8.2: Declining Computer Prices
US Bureau of Economic Analysis "Industry Spending on Capital Equipment." Aug. 27, 2004. http://www.bea.gov/bea/dn/comp-gdp.xls (September 2004).

8.3: Storage Cost of Information Exponentially Dropped, 1988–2002
Lyman and Varian "How much information?" 2000. http://www.sims.berkeley.edu/research/projects/how-much-info/how-much-info.pdf (September 2004).

8.4: Internet Domain Server Host Count Worldwide
Internet Software Consortium "Internet Domain Survey Host Count Worldwide." http://www.isc.org/ds/ (September 2004).

8.5: Use of Computer, Internet/E-mail at Work in the U.S.
See 8.1

8.6: Industry Spending on Capital Equipment Soared in the Last Decade
See 8.2

CHAPER NINE: BIOTECHNOLOGY

1. The Pew Initiative on Food and Biotechnology "Genetically Modified Crops in the United States." August 2004. http://pewagbiotech.org/resources/factsheets/display.php3?FactsheetID=2 (September 2004).

2. McHuhen, Alan "Contrast in the International Risk Debate Schemes." The 7th International Symposium on the Biosafety of Genetically Modified Organisms. International Society for Biosafety Research. October 2002.

3. Christensen, Jon "Golden Rice in a Grenade Proof House." The New York Times. Nov. 21, 2000.

4. Kennedy, Natel and Shetty "The Scourge of 'Hidden Hunger' Global Dimensions of Micronutrient Deficiencies." www.fao.org/DOCREP/005/y8346m/y8346m02.htm (September 2004).

5. The Oak Ridge National Laboratory "Human Genome Project Information." http://www.ornl.gov/TechResources/Human_Genome/medicine/medicine.html (September 2004).

6. The Office of Biotechnology Iowa State University "Biotechnology Information Series." http://www.biotech.iastate.edu/biotech_info_series/bio10.html (September 2004).

7. "Of Famine and Food Aid: BM Food Internationally." The Pew Initiative on Food and Biotechnology. http://pewagbiotech.org/buzz/display.php3?StoryID=77 (September2004).

8. "FDA Evaluation of Complaints Linked to Food Allegedly Containing Starlink Corn." Center for Food Safety and Applied Nutrition, The Environmental Protection Agency. June 13, 2001. http://www.epa.gov/scipoly/sap/2001/july/fda.pdf (September 2004).

GRAPHS

9.1: Biotechnology and The Modern Man

9.2: Increase in Global Area of Biotech Crops
The Pew Initiative on Food and Biotechnology "Genetically Modified Crops in the United States." August 2004. http://pewagbiotech.org/resources/factsheets/display.php3?FactsheetID=2 (September 2004).

9.3: Adoption of Genetically Engineered Crops in USA
Fernandez and McBride "Adoption of genetically engineered crops in USA." International Market Research Reports. http://biotech.about.com (September 2004).

9.4: Percent of Total Land Area Planted in Biotechnology Varieties by Country
James, Clive "Global Status of Commercialized Transgenic Crops: 2003." International Service for the Acquisition of Agri-biotech Applications (ISAAA). http://www.isaaa.org/Publications/briefs/briefs_30.htm (Sep 2004).

CHAPTER TEN: NANOTECHNOLOGY

1. Merckle, Ralph "Nanotechnology." Zyvex. http://www.zyvex.com/nano/ (September 2004).

2. Uldrich, Jack and Newberry, Deb. "The Next Big Thing Is Really Small: How Nanotechnology Will Change The Future Of Your Business." New York, Random House, Inc., 2003.

3. "GE Opens Technology Center in Germany." GE Press Release. June 28, 2004. www.ge.com/en/company/news/press/tec_ctr_germany.htm (September 2004).

4. National Science Foundation "Government Nanotechnology Funding: An International Outlook." June 30, 2003 http://www.nano.gov/html/res/IntlFundingRoco.htm (September 2004).
5. OECD "Nanotech is not Small." OECD Observer. Sept. 1, 2004. www.oecdobserver.org/news/fullstory/php/ai/1293/Nanotech_is_not_small.htm (September 2004).

6. Hassan, Emmauel and Sheehan, Jerry. "Scaling-Up Nanotechnology." Directorate for Science, Technology and Industry. OECD Observer. Oct. 17,2003. www.oecdobsrver.org/news/fullstory/php/ai/1005/scaling_up_nanotechnology.html (September 2004).

7. Rotman, David "Nanotech Goes to Work." Technology Review. Cambridge: Jan/Feb 2001. Vol 104, Iss 1; pg 62.

8. Roco, Mihail and Bainbridge, William Sims, eds. "Societal Implications of Nanoscience and Nanotechnology." National Science Foundation. March 2001. www.wtec.org/loyola/nano/NSET.Societal.Implications/nanosi.pdf (September 2004).

9. National Science Foundation "Government Nanotechnology Funding: An International Outlook." June 30, 2003 http://www.nano.gov/html/res/IntlFundingRoco.htm (September 2004).

10. Cardiff University "Nanomedicines." www.cardiff.ac.uk/community/healtofnation/advanceprospects/nano.html (September 2004).

11. Merckle, Ralph "Nanotechnology." Zyvex. http://www.zyvex.com/nano/ (September 2004).

12. Krane, Jim. "Fast Moving Nanotechnology Could Help the Environment." The Associated Press, Environmental News Network,. Sept. 6, 2002. http://www.enn.com/news/wire-stories/2002/09/09062002/ap_48365.asp (September 2004).

13. National Nanotechnology Initiative "Frequently Asked Questions." www.nano.gov/html/facts/faqs.html (September 2004).

14. Pethokookis, James "Small Tech and the Big Board." U.S. News and World Reports Sept. 25, 2003. www.usnews.com/usnews/tech/nextnews/archive/next030925.htm (September 2004).

GRAPHS

10.1: Estimated Government Nanotechnology R&D Expenditures, 1997-2003
Hassan, Emmauel and Sheehan, Jerry. "Scaling-Up Nanotechnology." Directorate for Science, Technology and Industry. OECD Observer. Oct. 17,2003. www.oecdobsrver.org/news/fullstory/php/ai/1005/scaling_up_nanotechnology.html (September 2004).

CHAPTER ELEVEN: CONFLICT

1. "Greed for Diamonds and Other 'Lootable' Commodities Fuels Civil Wars." The World Bank Group http://web.worldbank.org/WBSITE/EXTERNAL/NEWS/0,,contentMDK:20020847~menuPK:34459~pagePK:64003015~piPK:64003012~theSitePK:4607,00.html (October 2004).

2. "GDP per Capita for Various Years." Nationmaster.com (October 2004).

3. "JFK on Nuclear Weapons and Non-Proliferation." Waging Peace.Org, Nov. 17, 2003. http://www.waging-peace.org/articles/2003/11/17_carnegie_jfk-nuclear.htm (October 2004).

4. Hayes, Harry. "The Costs of Terrorism." International Review. Jan. 29, 2002. http://www.geocities.com/Paris/Rue/4637/terr25a.html (October 2004).

5. "The Costs of Terrorism" Asia Pacific Economic Cooperation: Submitted by Australia, 2003/SOMI/04. February 2003. http://www.apecsec.org.sg/apec/apec_groups/som_special_task_groups/counter_terrorism.download-links.0007.LinkURL.Download.ver5.1.9 (October 2004).
6. "The Costs of Terrorism" Asia Pacific Economic Cooperation: Submitted by Australia, 2003/SOMI/04. February 2003. http://www.apecsec.org.sg/apec/apec_groups/som_special_task_groups/counter_terrorism.download-links.0007.LinkURL.Download.ver5.1.9 (October 2004).

7. Hamblen, Mark. "Clinton Commits $1.46B to Fight Cyberterrorism." Jan. 26, 1999. http://www.cnn.com/TECH/computing/9901/26/clinton.idg/ (October 2004).

Graphs

11.1: Trend of International and Internal Conflicts
Alstrohm, C. "Casualties of Conflict." Geneva: ICRC 1991; SIPRI Yearbook 1991-1994: OxfordUniversity Press (October 2004).

11.2: Possible Areas of Internal Conflict through 2025
Director of Central Intelligence, Central Intelligence Agency. www.ocdi.gov (October 2004).

11.3: GDP Per Capita
Nationmaster.com: GDP per capita for various years. (October 2004).

11.4 Conflict and Country Wealth
 "Global Conflict Trends." http://members.aol.com/CSPmgm/conflict.htm#method (October 2004).

11.5: States of Concern and Their Suspected Weapons Capabilities
Pike, John. "States Possessing, Pursuing or Capable of Acquiring Weapons of Mass Destruction." Federation of American Scientists. July 2000. http://www.fas.org/irp/threat/wmd_state.htm (October 2004).

11.6: Possible Terrorism Activities Through 2025
See 11.2

CHAPTER TWELVE: GOVERNANCE

1. U.S. Department of State, United States Embassy, Bogotá, Colombia. http://usembassy.state.gov/colombia/wwwsfyi7.shtml (September 2004).

2. Lord Desai, Lord Judd and Sir John Thomson. "Global Governance: Yes, But What, Who and How?" Overseas Development Institute. 1998. http://www.odi.org.uk/speeches/govmt1.html (September 2004).

3. Lord Desai, Lord Judd and Sir John Thomson. "Global Governance: Yes, But What, Who and How?" Overseas Development Institute. 1998. http://www.odi.org.uk/speeches/govmt1.html (September 2004).

4. White, Peter & Buyle, Beatrijs. "Corporate Social Opportunity: Seven Steps to Make Corporate Social Responsibility Work for Your Business." Green Leaf. 2004.

5. "Democracy's Century, a Survey of Global Political Change in the 20th Century." http://www.freedomhouse.org/reports/century.html (September 2004).

6. "Understanding the World Trade Organizations." World Trade Organization. http://www.wto.org/english/thewto_e/whatis_e/tif_e/org6_e.htm (September 2004).

7. Fukuyama, Francis. "The End of History and the Last Man." Penguin. 1992. Introduction available at http://www.marxists.org/reference/subject/philosophy/works/us/fukuyama.htm (September 2004).

8. "Intellectual Property: Protection and Enforcement." World Trade Organization. http://www.wto.org/english/thewto_e/whatis_e/tif_e/org6_e.htm (September 2004).

9. Samuelson, Robert J. "The Foundations of Economic Development." Global Policy Forum. 2001. http://www.globalpolicy.org/socecon/develop/2001/0302cult.htm (September 2004).

10. Samuelson, Robert J. "The Foundations of Economic Development." Global Policy Forum. 2001. http://www.globalpolicy.org/socecon/develop/2001/0302cult.htm (September 2004).

11. The Institute for Policy Studies, Report on "The Rise of Corporate Global Power." http://www.ips-

dc.org/reports/top200.htm (September 2004).

12. Shah, Anup. "Corporations and Worker's Rights." Corporations. 2004.
http://www.globalissues.org/TradeRelated/Corporations/Labor.asp (September 2004).

13. Keller Rohrback. "Exxon Valdez." Seattle Class Action. http://www.seattleclassaction.com/exxon/exxon.asp
(September 2004).

GRAPHS

12.1: Number of Non-Governmental Organizations, 1951-2001
United Nations Conference on Trade and Development, 2001 World Investment Report (http://www.unc-tad.org): extracted from http://www.globalpolicy.org/socecon/tncs/tables.htm (September 2004).

For More Information:

Asia Times Online "Special Reports: The 2015 World, According to the CIA." Jan. 25, 2001.
http://www.atimes.com/reports/CA24Ai01.html (September 2004).

CSIS "Health: HIV/AIDS." http://www.globalization101.org/issue/health/21.asp (September 2004).

Deame, Laura. "A Generation of Orphans: Another Challenge for AIDS-Ravaged Countries." World
Resources Institute. May 2001. http://earthtrends.wri.org/text/POP/features/POP_fea_orphans.htm
(September 2004).

Ecoworld, Global Environmental Company "Energy."
http://www.ecoworld.org/energy/EcoWorld_Energy_Articles.cfm (September 2004).

Food and Agriculture Organization (FAO) of the United Nations. www.fao.org (September 2004).

The Foresight Institute "Nanotechnology." http://www.foresight.org/NanoRev (September 2004).

Genetically Engineered Food "GE Technologies Will Solve World Hunger."
http://www.globalissues.org/EnvIssues/GEFood/Hunger.asp (September 2004).

Global Reach "Global Internet Statistics (By Language)." http://www.glreach.com/globstats/ (September
2004).

House Committee on Science "Molecular Manufacturing: Societal Implications of Advanced
Nanotechnology." http://www.house.gov/science/hearings/full03/apr09/peterson.htm (September 2004).

Hunter, Lori. "Chapter 3: Population Distribution: Trends & Environmental Implications." The
Environmental Implications of Population Dynamics. 2001.
http://www.rand.org/publications/MR/MR1191/MR1191.ch3.pdf (September 2004).

International Monetary Fund: World Economic Outlook, April 2004
http://www.imf.org/external/pubs/ft/weo/2004/01/ (September 2004).

Meldrum, Julian. "40 Million People Now Living with HIV." UNAIDS and WHO. Nov. 28, 2004.
http://www.aidsmap.com/news/newsdisplay2.asp?newsId=1318 (September 2004).
Mussa, Michael. "Factors Driving Global Economic Integration." Economic Counselor and Director of
Research, IMF. http://www.imf.org/external/np/speeches/2000/082500.htm (September 2004).

Nakagomi, Yasuko. "A Comparative Study on Population Growth, Urban Expansion and Environmental
Degradation in Mega-Cities."
http://www.es.a.u-tokyo.ac.jp/lep/thesis/98M_nakagomi-e.html (September 2004).

National Center for Policy Analysis "Social Policy." http://www.ncpa.org/pd/social/sociala.html (September 2004).

National Council on Economic Education "Population Growth: Friend or Foe?" http://www.econedlink.org/lessons/index.cfm?lesson=EM32 (September 2004).

National Nanotechnology Initiative. http://nano.gov (September 2004).

"People on the Move: Urbanization and International Migration." International Planned Parenthood Federation. http://www.ippf.org/resource/6billion/urban.htm (September 2004).

Perlman, Janice. "Mega-Cities Program: Shrinking World, Growing Cities." Trinity Reporter.Spring 2001. http://www.trincoll.edu/pub/reporter/Spring%202001/mega%20cities.shtml (September 2004).

Pew Center on Global Climate Change. www.pewclimate.org (September 2004).

Pew Initiative on Food and Biotechnology: www.pewagbiotech.org (September 2004).

Population Council "Population Today: Diverging Trends in Rich and Poor Countries." http://www.pop-council.org/pc50/articles/populationtoday.html (September 2004).

The Population Institute. http://www.populationinstitute.org (September 2004).

Population Reference Bureau. "Population Bulletin: Facing the HIV/AIDS Pandemic." http://www.fhi.org/NR/rdonlyres/etjfi5cfbmerdt7ft6gz7oebxvixgrsfwweiv57utmsrv6dwdidsslxhpcizthx-naaxa4kpge5fbvd/FacingAIDSPandeme.pdf (September 2004).

"Reaching the Unreached: Challenges for the 21st Century: Challenges in Indian Mega Cities" 22nd WEDC Conference: Discussion Paper. 1996. http://www.lboro.ac.uk/departments/cv/wedc/papers/22/groupa/shuk-la.pdf (September 2004).

Shukla and Romaprasad. "Indian Urban Transport: Vision 2050" Terra Green. Jan. 15, 2003. http://www.teriin.org/terragreen/issue28/essay.htm (September 2004).

"Special Report on Sustainable Development in Asian Cities." Asia Energy News. 2001. http://aen.ceerd.net/archive/2001/aen_0701a.htm (September 2004).

The Union of International Associations. http://www.uia.org (September 2004).

United Nations Convention on Climate Change. www.unfcc.int (September 2004).

United Nations Environmental Programme. www.unep.org (September 2004).

The United Nations Programme on Ageing. http://www.un.org/esa/socdev/ageing/ (September 2004).

U. S. Census Bureau. "World POPClock Projection.". http://www.census.gov/cgi-bin/ipc/popclockw (September 2004).

The World Bank Group. "HIV/AIDS & Development." http://www1.worldbank.org/hiv_aids/ (September 2004).

World Health Organization. "SARS: Breaking the Chains of Transmission." 2003. http://www.who.int/features/2003/07/en/ (September 2004).

ABOUT THE AUTHORS

DR. FARIBORZ GHADAR, the William A. Schreyer Chair of Global Management and director of the Center for Global Business Studies at Penn State University, is an authority on future business trends, global economic assessment, and global corporate strategy and implementation. He consults with major corporations, governments, and government agencies, and regularly conducts executive programs for multinational corporations.

Professor Ghadar holds a Ph.D. in business from Harvard Graduate School of Business Administration. He also holds two master's degrees, an M.B.A. from Harvard and a M.S. in mechanical engineering from Massachusetts Institute of Technology, and two B.S. degrees from MIT, one in biomedical engineering and one in chemical engineering.

Dr. Ghadar held a vice-ministerial post in Iran during the Shah's regime, served as an investment banker at the International Finance Corporation at the World Bank group, and was the research coordinator of the Harvard Multinational Enterprise Project. *BusinessWeek* named Dr. Ghadar one of the top 10 "Stars of Finance," and he was selected as one of the top 10 thought leaders and practitioners of strategy coaching in *Profiles in Coaching: The 2004 Handbook of Best Practices in Leadership Coaching*.

Professor Ghadar is the author of more than 10 books, including *Financing Growth in Developing Economies* and *New Information Technology and Its Impact on Global Business Management*. He frequently is quoted in internationally circulated publications and has been a featured speaker and an interviewee on major television networks and business broadcasts.

MR. ERIK R. PETERSON is senior vice president at the Center for Strategic and International Studies (CSIS), where he is also the William A. Schreyer Chair in Global Analysis. He is also director of the Global Strategy Institute at CSIS. Mr. Peterson specializes in geopolitical and country risk assessment, international trade and finance, and international business strategy and global strategic planning. He consults regularly with senior leaders in both government and business on over-the-horizon issues. His "Seven Revolutions" initiative — an effort to scan strategic global trends out to the year 2025 — is in strong demand by senior leaders in government and business around the world.

Mr. Peterson came to the Center from Kissinger Associates, where he was director of research. He holds an M.B.A. in international finance from the Wharton School at the University of Pennsylvania, an M.A. in international law and economics from the School of Advanced International Studies at the Johns Hopkins University, and a B.A. from Colby College. He holds the Certificate of Eastern European Studies from the University of Fribourg in Switzerland and the Certificate in International Legal Studies from The Hague Academy of International Law in the Netherlands.

Mr. Peterson has lectured on international economics and finance and geopolitical risk at numerous colleges and universities, including Penn State, Chapman University, George Mason University, Georgia Tech, and the Wharton School. He has been a fellow of the World Economic Forum, a member of the advisory board of the Global Capital Markets Center at Duke University, and a member of the Council on Foreign Relations. Currently, he is a member of the advisory board of the Center for the Study of the Presidency, and a board member of the Center for Global Business Studies at Penn State.